לה׳ הארץ ומלואה
ר׳ אלימלך בן ציון רכס
Rabbi Michael Reches
410-486-8991
mreches@btfiloh.org

CUTTING

UNDERSTANDING AND OVERCOMING

SELF-MUTILATION

CUTTING

UNDERSTANDING

AND

OVERCOMING

SELF-MUTILATION

STEVEN LEVENKRON

W. W. NORTON AND COMPANY

NEW YORK/LONDON

For information about permission to reproduce selections from this book,
write to Permissions, W. W. Norton & Company, Inc.,
500 Fifth Avenue, New York, NY 10110.

The text of this book is composed in Bembo wtih the display set in Stencil Sans
and Futura Bold. Composition and Manufacturing by The Haddon Craftsmen, Inc.
Book design by JAM Design

Library of Congress Cataloging-in-Publication Data

Levenkron, Steven, 1941–
Cutting : understanding and overcoming self-mutilation / Steven Levenkron.
p.   cm.
Includes bibliographical references and index.
ISBN 0-393-02741-4
1. Self-mutilation—Popular works.   I. Title.
RC552.S4L48   1998
616.85'82—dc21   98–10274
CIP

W. W Norton & Company, Inc., 500 Fifith Avenue, New York, N.Y. 10110
http://www.wwnorton.com

W. W. Norton & Company Ltd., 10 Coptic Street, London WC1A 1PU

1   2   3   4   5   6   7   8   9   0

*For my wife and lifetime partner in
all things, including this work,
Abby Levenkron*

CONTENTS

PREFACE

As a modern society, we have become inured to watching open-heart surgery and emergency-room procedures on television. With the help of our own experiences and the information provided by modern media, we now casually discuss gynecological problems, childbirth, cancer, organ transplants, and so on.

Yet we still shrink from acknowledging the signs of emotional and mental pain. This book takes a look at the difficult subject of self-mutilation: how it relates to our society, and our fear of the dark impulses that lurk within us all.

Until 1996, the public had little familiarity with self-mutilation. Then Princess Diana volunteered that she had been a cutter, and articles on the topic began to appear in popular magazines.

Often I meet new patients who say that they already have tried several therapists before coming to me. As soon as they indicate that they are self-mutilators, the therapists respond that they have no experience and decline to treat them. Why hasn't this disorder been looked at more carefully in the past? Perhaps because such pathological behavior is as repellent to the psychological community as it is to the general public.

Back in 1974, when I first treated anorexics, my colleagues, most of them psychiatrists, tried to dissuade me. "Steve," they would say, "specializing in treating anorexics would be like having an entire practice of suicidal patients." Coping with anorexics was considered foolish and frightening at a time when a therapist could seek out a patient population who simply wanted to be analyzed—to lie on a couch and free-associate about their childhoods. Over the past twenty-four years, an entire subdivision of the profession has sprung up to research and treat eating disorders.

Yet, aside from the current publicity, most of which is sensational, unhealthily explicit, and serves only to frighten and disgust people, we are still largely in the dark about the phenomenon of self-mutilation. Much research remains to be done. Our primary source of information will be those people who have engaged in this behavior in the past and those that are doing it in the present: the patients themselves.

The mental health profession (whether its members have medical or nonmedical backgrounds) will have to get comfortable talking with patients, in detail, about cutting and burning oneself. They will have to get used to demanding that their patients show them the damage done, inspect this damage, and determine whether or not a physician needs to treat them. All of this must become a natural and comfortable part of the therapist's treatment repertoire. It requires, in most cases, knowledge equivalent to the medical information found in the *Boy Scout Manual*.

When therapists first began to treat eating disorders, they had to learn about electrolytic imbalance, heart rate, blood pressure, body temperature, blood values, and organ function, as well as estrogen levels and their relationship to menstruation, and weight-to-height ratios. Suddenly, therapists were talking with their patients about intimate details of bodily function. This was something that had rarely occurred in previous therapies. These are patients who are mystified by their bodies and who deliberately distort their physical appearance. They need therapists who, as their teachers, will feel as comfortable and knowledgeable about their patients' bodies as their minds.

The therapist who chooses to work with self-mutilators will have to become desensitized not only to the results of the physical acts committed against the body but to the fact that this damage is *self-inflicted*. I suspect it is this aspect that is the hardest for us all to deal with.

ACKNOWLEDGMENTS

I would like to acknowledge the enormous help given to me by my editor at Norton, Jill Bialosky, who has labored relentlessly on behalf of myself and the reader to make this book as comprehensive and understandable as possible. Also Ann Adelman for her thorough and painstaking copyediting and valuable suggestions.

I would also like to acknowledge the assistance of my daughter Gabrielle Levenkron in preparing the first draft of this work. And I must thank my agent of twenty years, Olga B. Wieser, at Wieser and Wieser, for her invaluable assistance and advice.

PART

I

THE
ILLNESS

INTRODUCTION

One evening, many years ago, I received a call from a seventeen-year-old patient I was treating for depression and feelings of alienation. The voice at the other end of the phone was hollow, drowsy, expressionless.

"Hello. This is Eileen.★ My little sister won't stop crying."

"Why is she crying?" I prompted.

"She's crying because I'm cutting my hand with a kitchen knife and it's bleeding a lot and I won't stop."

She sounded almost bored reporting this to me. I had no concept of what her behavior or tone meant. In my ignorance (and some alarm), I reverted to my practical Boy Scout training.

"How long is the cut?"

"There are three of them, about one inch each," she responded in the same hollow tone.

★All the names in this book have been changed and situations disguised to protect patient confidentiality.

"How deep have you cut?"

"Not so deep. Maybe an eighth of an inch, or a little more."

She was becoming a little more responsive.

"I would like you to wash the cuts with soap and water, dry them, and put hydrogen peroxide on them; that will stop the bleeding. Then I want you to place Band-Aids very tightly across each one and call me back when this is done."

She responded compliantly. "Okay."

Half an hour later she called me back, announcing, "I did what you said to."

"Do the cuts hurt?"

"A little."

"Has your sister stopped crying?"

"Yes."

"How old is she?"

"Seven."

"When will your parents return?"

"Probably very late."

"It's ten now. Why don't you put her to bed. After that, go to bed yourself and we'll talk about this tomorrow. I'd like you to come in right after school at three-thirty."

"Okay."

This "Okay" was a little more expressive than the zombie voice earlier. That was a good sign, but I certainly needed to think, and to consult with colleagues about this strange behavior before I spoke with Eileen again.

I have been treating self-mutilators since 1976. As I saw more instances of patients cutting or burning their own skin, I maintained my Boy Scout stance. I rationalized that my main concern was figuring out what this behavior meant to them so that I could help them understand and overcome it. They all gave me different hypothetical reasons for their actions.

I was soon shocked to discover how often psychiatrists encountered this behavior in their patients. And yet their reactions were, for the most part, almost as casual as Eileen's had been.

"Oh yeah," I'd hear, "another cutter. They're pretty sick cookies."

"Sick cookies?" I thought. Were they simply writing their patients off as hopelessly mentally ill? For me, the patients' behavior was a clue to the severity of their emotional disturbances, and maybe to the severity of the *causes* of those disturbances.

Today, cutting is a behavior found all too often among the emotionally disturbed or mentally ill, but one that still has been avoided by professionals and the public alike.

My purpose in devoting a whole book to one type of pathological behavior is threefold: first, to invite its victims to come out from their emotional hiding places and disclose who they are; second, to encourage more interest (and discourage revulsion) on the part of the mental health community so that more research will be done; and lastly, to help those afflicted, their families, friends, and the general public to see this behavior for what it is. Self-mutilation is a frightening barrier that keeps us from seeing a person who is lost, in pain, and in desperate need of help.

Cutting takes the reader through the psychological experience of the person who seeks relief from mental pain and anguish in self-inflicted physical pain; the person who finds solace in the letting of her own blood. In the same way that anorexia and bulimia manifested in behaviors that seemed at first incomprehensible to the public, later to be explained by patiently examining these apparently bizarre behaviors, the behaviors of the self-mutilator are similarly unraveled step by step. Although some of these strategies are directed toward the therapist, any way that the parent can augment this therapeutic style will hasten recovery.

At this time we are woefully short on statistics, but it is inferred that the percentage of cutters in our society is similar to those who have anorexia, one in every two hundred and fifty girls.⋆ The number of those who have permanently impaired themselves as a result of a self-mutilating act is equally difficult to determine. And the death rate is blurred by our inability to distinguish between those diagnosed as suicides versus accidental death from self-mutilation. The language of this book reflects the fact that so many more girls than boys manifest these behaviors. However, I want to stress that boys, too, can be at risk.

Self-injury is not a new phenomenon. There are numerous historical accounts of self-flagellation, for example, promoted apparently to relieve religious guilt. Christian flagellants, both clergy and laity, have flogged themselves as a means of penance since shortly after the death of Christ. In the mid-thirteenth century, flagellant brotherhoods composed of laymen and women as well as clergy arose in Italy, and the practice spread into Germany and the Low Countries. The scourge of the Black Death increased the fear of guilt and sin, yet by the fourteenth century the moral corruption of the church made it impossible for many religiously sensitive people to turn there for relief. Flagellants sought by their own efforts to mitigate the divine judgment that was felt to be at hand, forming groups that traveled about the country on foot.

In reading these accounts, one can see a parallel between failed faith or trust in the church and the failure of trust in one's own family in contemporary life. Perhaps we are talking about a universal defense mechanism to which people have always resorted in order to avoid a sense of dread—whether in terms of believing themselves literally damned or feeling emotionally tormented.

The greatest fear we all carry within us is the fear of self. We

---

⋆Based on an informal survey by the Canadian Broadcasting Company, in which five hundred school psychologists were asked if they had seen cutters in the last year. They indicated an incidence of two to three cutters per school.

worry about losing our temper, about our violence emerging and hurting others—especially those we love the most. Regularly in television and newspaper accounts we learn of husbands beating or murdering their wives, of parents beating or killing their children. Such news sends a shudder through us all. We don't want to believe that members of our own species are capable of such terrible acts.

Just as we fear the human potential for violence against others, we may also fear the possible impulse to hurt ourselves. When we see the wounds or scars of a cutter, do we, just for an instant, fear that we could harm our own skin by attacking it with a sharp instrument? The act of deliberately causing oneself to bleed frightens us in many complicated and varied ways. Clearly, people who harm or inadvertently kill themselves create in us a very uncomfortable mix of fear, guilt, anger, and frustration.

In order to understand and treat self-mutilators, we have to understand enough about ourselves so that we can become effective in helping those who feel abandoned, without confusing our own fears with theirs. Each of these self-harming people has a different history, a different motive, a different state of mind before, during, and after harming themselves. As their helpers, we will have to overcome our own feelings of discomfort. This book proposes to take the mystery out of the frightening phenomenon known as "self-mutilation."

1

WHAT IS SELF-MUTILATION?

The consensus of several dictionary definitions describes mutilation as "the act of damaging seriously by cutting off, or altering an essential part." In most cases of self-mutilation, the "essential part" of the self that is damaged is the skin, which is cut with a knife or razor blade, or scraped with an abrasive material—scissors, bottle cap, etc. Sometimes the skin is burned. In the course of treating self-mutilators, I have seen what a hot teakettle, a match, or a lit cigarette can do to the flesh. Sometimes the skin is chafed with detergent or other irritating chemicals.

The damage is rarely life-threatening, and the location of the wounds is usually on an easily hidden part of the body, though not always. Since it is the skin that is damaged, and not veins, arteries, tendons, or ligaments, the long-term harm is usually restricted to scarring.

Nonetheless, self-mutilation is a truly gruesome behavior accompanied by cosmetically gruesome results. It is the extreme nature of these external acts of self-harm that causes us to consider them worthy of psychological examination, and urges us to uncover the mental and emotional desperation they suggest.

It is important to understand that these forms of self-mutilation are not part of group rituals, not just an adolescent trend. They represent, rather, individual psychopathology: mental illness. For the purposes of this book, the current trend of piercing the skin on various parts of the face and body, ranging from the ears to the nose, nipples, navel, genitals, eyebrows, and tongue, is not self-mutilation. This behavior, although repugnant to some of us, falls into the category of adolescent trendiness (which also includes larger and more outrageous tattoos). Although such behavior alone does not constitute psychopathology in an individual, it may however create psychopathology in his or her parents.

The reason I distinguish between similar behaviors—one "sick" and the other "goofy"—is that their origins stand in sharp contrast. The "sick" behavior is a manifestation of severe psychological illness, whereas the "goofy" behavior complies with certain socially accepted norms. There are significant differences in the psychological motivation behind the respective actions of each group, as well as in the actual experience of the individual who alters his or her skin.

An analogy to conventional dieting versus anorexia nervosa is useful here. When most of us diet, we feel deprived, annoyed. When the anorexic is starving herself, she feels satisfaction, even though she is suffering pain and may be in danger of losing her life.

When someone decides to pierce or tattoo a part of his or her body, he or she feels pain, and dislikes it. Some people even do it feeling terrified, but it's a package deal: if you want the tattoo, you have to endure the pain. When the self-mutilator cuts herself, on the other hand, she is usually in a trance state, seeking out the pain and blood. She is far less concerned with the resulting change her skin will undergo. Self-mutilators are not acting within the norms of any cultural microcosm; they do not plan their activity, but rather are overtaken by a compulsion to commit these acts, which are not about conscious intent. For the self-mutilator, it is the *experience* of physical pain—for its calming effect on her more painful psychological state—that is being sought.

In the Introduction, I described a seventeen-year-old girl who called to tell me her sister wouldn't stop crying. You'll recall Eileen, my patient, told me that her younger sister was crying because Eileen was cutting her own hand with a knife and it was bleeding. Eileen was baby-sitting for her sister at the time. You may also recall that her tone was flat, disengaged. It was almost as if she were watching a boring movie and commenting on it. Her style of reporting did not at all reflect the actual nature of the situation. Her voice did not resonate as that of a girl who was drawing her own blood with a kitchen knife.

We might say that Eileen was out of touch with reality at the time, certainly the reality of her responsibility to her younger sister. She was also out of touch with the reality of her actions, and with her feelings about what she was doing to herself. Eileen was in fact devoid of any emotional response to what was going on.

Regardless of whether we term Eileen's condition as being **out of touch with reality, psychotic**, or **in a dissociated state**, the scene constitutes severely disturbed psychiatric behavior. This is the element that must be present in order to meet the criteria for **self-mutilation** as I define the term in this book. "Severely disturbed behavior" does not mean hopeless, but it does mean that it will take a long time, lots of focused attention, and an intense emotional bond between helper and sufferer in order to repair the damage.

At present, self-mutilation is not officially recognized as a disorder and is therefore not listed in the fourth edition of the

Diagnostic and Statistical Manual of Mental Disorders.★ Though briefly mentioned as a behavior sometimes seen in borderline personality disorders, it is cited only in its capacity as a feature of a larger disorder. When I use the terms **feature** and **disorder** in this book, I am treating self-mutilation in the same way that obsessive-compulsive disorders (especially **trichotillomania** or the pulling out of one's hair) are treated in the diagnostic literature.

In the most severely pathological forms, self-mutilation can be classified using the following diagnostic criteria:

- Recurrent cutting or burning of one's skin.
- A sense of tension present immediately before the act is committed.
- Relaxation, gratification, pleasant feelings, and numbness experienced concomitant with the physical pain.
- A sense of shame and fear of social stigma, causing the individual to attempt to hide scars, blood, or other evidence of the acts of self-harm.

Of course, what is not mentioned here (and usually isn't in the psychiatric definitions) is "Why does such disordered behavior happen?" "What does it mean?" and "What does it tell us about other coexisting personality or mood disorders?"

As in the case of so many other disorders, and features of those disorders, the answer to these questions is that we won't know without understanding much more of the individual than just these acts of cutting or self-harming alone.

★This failure on the part of the *Diagnostic and Statistical Manual* to consider a severe, physically endangering, and sometimes life-threatening psychological behavior as a disorder means that clinical efforts to understand the problem are in danger of remaining on the back burner. For victims and their families, this means that most who suffer will continue to do so.

Our first task, then, is to interpret the act of self-mutilation. Is it a love of pain? Does the cutter *enjoy* pain? Is this like **masochism**, where the pain alone is the end in and of itself? No. Self-mutilating behavior is different. We have to put ourselves inside the head of a cutter to comprehend the personal value and meanings that pain holds for her. Let's use another patient's report of her experiences as an example.

Annika's Story

"I was home alone. There was something both wonderful and terrible about the privacy. I walked from room to room, glad that each one was empty. No one could nag me, bother me, or scare me. I was feeling safe. After an hour of looking at magazines, I started to feel frightened of nothing in particular. I wanted the fear to go away. I tried to tell myself that there was nothing wrong; school was okay, my oboe playing was good, I had parties to go to. But the fear wouldn't go away. I banged my forehead against the wall of my bedroom. My head stung, but only for a moment. As the stinging diminished, I knew that I needed something that would last much longer. It had to last so long that by the time it went away, my feeling of dread would be gone and wouldn't come back, at least for a long time.

"I left my bedroom and went into the kitchen. No sneaking around this time. I would look at the knives on the rack as if I were shopping in a department store, leisurely. No sneaking into a stall in the ladies' room with a small sewing scissors this time. I could feel the fear refusing to leave me, but I knew I could get rid of it at any second. I chose the sharp serrated knife we use for frozen foods. The serrations would make the most jagged, roughest cuts of all. It would hurt the most, bleed the most, and take the longest time to heal. I would make the cut slowly, getting the most pain from each millimeter.

"I placed it across my left forearm on the underside—easy to hide. Easy to explain as an accident from a fall. I slowly made a one-inch cut. I thought I could feel each tooth of the knife's edge bite into and tear a little piece of skin.

"It wasn't pain I was feeling, it was like an injection of Novocaine that the dentist uses; it makes pain go away even though the needle 'pricks' as the dentist puts it in. And because I controlled the pain, there was no fear with it. So maybe it's not real pain. When I finished the inch, blood ran down the side of my forearm in a neat stream onto a folded paper towel. The stream was dark red and thick, but I wanted to see more, so I tilted my arm and the stream broke into three rivulets and the rivulets broke into a wash that was three inches wide and turned my forearm red.

"That was enough for me to see. The fear and dread were gone. I washed my arm under cold water from the tap and used hydrogen peroxide to stop the bleeding. I put a gauze pad on with adhesive tape. I went back to my bed and fell asleep. It took me two hours to remember the details, though I knew what I had done when I woke up in the morning."

I could see Annika's mood change as she recounted this incident. As she was describing the cutting and bleeding, she went into a trancelike state as if she were reliving it all. This kind of trancelike state is typical of cutters. I asked Annika to tell me what the experience meant to her, its value. She said, "It was like medicine for my fears."

———————

Annika's explanation made me wonder why it was that inflicting pain on herself and causing herself to bleed felt like medicine; why it felt like caring for herself. Most self-mutilators give similar explanations about the "rewards" of such behavior. This suggests that somewhere in the past, pain was somehow connected to the idea of home and comfort. These kinds of associations—pain with comfort—are alien to most of us.

It is important to remember that people will generally seek the familiar, the repetitious, rather than what is new and constructive.

If the familiar happens to be painful or harmful, that rarely stops someone from seeking it out. Otherwise we would never do what is not in our own best interest—especially during those times when we are *aware* that it's not—with regard to our own health, welfare, financial well-being, and healthy relationships. When the familiar is grotesque, a person seeks out the grotesque. We call such behavior a **disorder**.

Shila's Story

Let's take the case of Shila, whose father stopped being close to and supportive of her when she reached puberty and developed breasts. As she hit adolescence, Shila's father backed away from her in terms of affection, communication, and conversation in general. He may have been under the impression that such interaction was inappropriate now that Shila was a teenager, but the result was that she felt both punished and abandoned by her father. In response, she dressed boyishly, avoided makeup, and did her cutting on her breasts, blaming her body and the onset of puberty for driving her father away.

The anxiety that Shila felt but couldn't identify was a result of her father's separation from her. Unconsciously attacking the cause of his unwitting abandonment was Shila's only means of quelling her fear. This behavior, and the feelings of abandonment that caused it, is not the sort of thing most teenagers can talk about, within the family or without. With no verbal outlet, Shila's behavior grew stronger, developing a life, an energy, and a rationale of its own.

Self-Injury as Protest

To help us further define what self-mutilation is, we can take a look at what does not constitute such behavior.

Maria acted out consciously on her family by holding her success and safety hostage in order to punish her overprotective parents. As long as she was sick, doing badly in school, having trouble with friends, she was rewarded with lots of supportive attention from her parents. The more care she received at home, the less equipped (and more afraid) to cope with anyone outside the family she became. At this point, Maria resented her parents *and* their love deeply.

When she was feeling this resentment, Maria would up the ante. She would feign illness, and when more care came (feeding into the cycle of her resentment), she would become more extreme, purposely falling down or even cutting herself. But her self-injury was a protest that she broadcast loudly to the rest of her family. She did not keep it a secret, hated doing it, and blamed everyone around her for her injury. Even her cutting was a conscious manipulation to frighten her family.

Maria had a hostile dependence on her family, which made her increasingly unfit to cope with the rest of the world, but because her behavior was directed at others, she was not a self-mutilator. Maria was atypical in the spectrum of self-mutilators; typical self-mutilators are not as consciously deliberate.

Diagnostic Factors

As we learn more about self-mutilators, new diagnostic subcategories may emerge, based on certain additional factors:

- other mental health problems;
- the frequency and severity of the acts of self-mutilation;
- internal versus external stress factors;
- the patient's state of mind when such acts are executed (i.e., whether or not the person is aware of what he/she is doing at the time); and

• the types of personality disorders that drive someone to commit these acts.

This type of understanding is crucial for determining the treatment that will be most helpful in each case, and the prognosis or chances for recovery.

2

THE PHENOMENON OF
A SELF-DESTRUCTIVE ACT

What does it feel like to cut yourself, deliberately, until you feel pain and start to bleed? Why would you do this? What does the experience of pain do to you, or for you? These are the questions that all self-mutilators ask themselves amid their desperation and shame. The answers come from many directions and have many meanings.

"Thanks, I really needed that"—we have all heard that sentence in movies and on television. Sometimes it's in a serious context, sometimes funny. It refers to when a person gets "carried away" in a particular situation, overreacting, becoming frantic and hysterical, and ultimately losing control. There is always a second person in the formula who slaps the out-of-control person quite hard in the face. The first person regains his composure and expresses his gratitude for the painful, distracting slap with this cliché.

Most of us find the example of the slap in the face both familiar and understandable; yet the concept of cutting into our own skin, of feeling relief at both the pain and the sight of blood, seems

totally alien to us. Relieving ourselves of pain is usually done with
the help of something tranquilizing or anesthetic, not more
painful. It seems paradoxical to utilize a greater pain for relief from
pain, paradoxical to use the sight of one's own blood for relief. Yet
that is precisely the mechanism of relief for those whose world is
one of choices between one kind of pain or another.

There are many explanations for how an individual develops
such peculiar and limited choices. But all consist of scenarios that
are radically different from most healthy childhood experiences,
feelings, and development.

As I've already stressed, we all seek the familiar. If we are lucky,
the familiar experiences of our past are pleasant, supportive, kind,
and caring. If we are unlucky, they are neglectful, insensitive, punishing, and abusive. As children, we are incapable of making judgments about the adults in our lives and how they treat us. We
never decide that our parents or primary caretakers are wrong. If
they are wrong, then we have no competent parents and are in effect abandoned. Fear of abandonment is the greatest fear a child
has. It far supersedes the fear of death, which, to a child, is an ab-
straction at best.

If a child could designate a parent's act as "wrong," then the
child would have to accept that he or she has an incompetent parent. This is the emotional equivalent to having no parent at all.
And because parents are a child's only protection, having no parent means losing that protection and its sense of safety.

If a child's experience with her parents is uncomfortable, neglectful, or painful, the child accepts the pain and assumes that her
parents' behavior is justified because they must be "right." She has
only herself to blame for the fault of failing to adjust to the pain,
because the pain must be right. Think, for example, of the verbally
abused child who is told that she's stupid and worthless. The
painful verbal abuse becomes familiar, reliable, part of home. As the
small child develops into an older child, an adolescent, and then a
young adult, she needs her parents' protection from the world less

and less. It is then *her* job to recreate the pain that guided her through her early life, the pain that means home, safety, comfort.

This is an example of a pathological distortion of the superego, or conscience. The child has grown into a young person whose associations and meanings for everything in her world have been malformed by her earliest experiences. Although most of us can only comprehend her mode of thinking as backwards, or messed up, it is in fact, tragically, the most logical result of her childhood.

The best way of understanding why a person would want to harm herself is by listening to the voices of those suffering from this disorder.

Jessica: Incest and Cutting

Jessica explained that she had a problem with "losing time," a temporary amnesia that would last two to three hours. This was especially dangerous because she was a nanny who took care of a three-year-old girl in an affluent suburb and had the responsibilities of driving the child to various activities. She was afraid that she would forget where she had left the little girl last, or not pick her up on time, thereby endangering both her own job and the child's safety.

Sometimes Jessica would "wake up" sitting behind the wheel of the car, parked on a country road, only to discover that she had "lost" two hours. She would have no idea what she had done for those two hours. She might have been acting responsibly, carrying out her caretaking duties, or sleeping, or involved in any sort of activity. She said that sometimes she "woke up" bleeding, not knowing how she had become injured.

During the course of treatment, Jessica revealed that her father had raped her from the age of five to the age of twelve. When she got her first period, he began to sodomize her so she couldn't get pregnant. This all ended when she was fourteen and threatened to tell school authorities about his behavior. Because Jessica's mother was severely alcoholic, she had never been a source of protection to her child.

In therapy, Jessica would occasionally make mention of "strange" and lengthy showers she was taking. Each time she alluded to this puzzling activity, she would promptly change the subject. At one point, after a year of therapy, she volunteered that she took these extended showers when she felt lonely or abandoned.

I believed that she was ready to go into more detail, so I asked her what was so "strange" about these showers. I had assumed that she was being compulsive about cleaning herself, perhaps to cleanse herself of feelings of contamination from her father's violation of her body. Her answer surprised me and led me to a different interpretation.

"I, um, use a lot of soap, liquid soap, all over my body, but not just on the outside. I use it on the inside, too. I rub the concentrated soap on the inside until it burns, and I keep rubbing until I've had enough burning and pain."

I responded, "It seems that you're not after the cleaning abilities of the soap but the pain-causing aspects of it."

She nodded in agreement.

"You describe the pain as burning?"

She nodded again.

"Does the burning inside you resemble the burning feeling that accompanied the stretching feeling you experienced as a little girl being raped by an adult man?"

She began to cry. "It's crazy! It's crazy! Yes, it does! Why would I want to make myself feel the feelings I hated the most when I was little?"

After handing her a box of tissues, I started slowly, "Who else was important to you, were you attached to when you were little?"

She blew her nose loudly. "No one! *She* was always drowsy-drunk on wine! There was no one else, just *him!*"

"Was he ever nice to you?"

She blew her nose loudly again. "Yes," she said grudgingly, "he took me to the park, he bought me candy. Once in a while he would take me to school. *She* never did."

"Is it possible that when you feel lonely, you recreate the feelings, pain and all, that remind you of him to relieve your loneliness?"

"That's so sick!"

"But it's home, or at least the only home you knew."

"That's not only sick, it's pathetic . . . I'm worthless. If he had been just my stepfather, it might mean I had some value. But I was flesh and blood and he trashed me. He hurt me. So all I have left for memories is pain in my body's openings." She sobbed for the rest of the session.

Jessica is an extreme example of how people are capable of revising the meaning of pain—from something to be avoided to something that is pursued and embraced. She anticipated her pain-inducing experiences with excitement because she knew that she would soon be escaping from her feelings of loneliness and abandonment. The pain she inflicted upon herself came as a welcome trade-off from the terrible feelings, and transported her away from her loneliness into a trance state where she was oblivious to her painful emotions. She had no *conscious* thoughts or feelings while she was hurting herself. *Unconsciously,* the pain connected her to her sole attachment, her father. Escaping her feelings of loneliness and abandonment while connecting herself with her only caregiver, no matter how sick and cruel he was, were the goals of Jessica's self-harm.

During her showers, Jessica would evoke states in herself that lasted for an hour or more. Other times she would have no memory of how the trancelike state had developed. She would simply experience a "waking-up" feeling and notice that she had new cuts and bruises on her body. She did not remember how they got there. It would seem that sometimes Jessica needed to deepen her trance state by causing herself physical pain.

Juanita's Story: "Bitter Medicine"

Juanita was a twenty-year-old student whose family moved from Mexico when she was five. Her father was an engineer who made a good income working for a chemical company. They lived in an affluent community in which her father was very sensitive to the anti-Hispanic feeling. Most Hispanic men there were day laborers, gardeners, and caretakers; he always dressed well, to avoid being confused with them. Juanita's mother was depressed. When she took her children (Juanita's three older brothers and two older sisters) to school, the other mothers initially assumed she was their nanny. If they spoke to her, it was to patronize her. She had to continually explain that she was a resident of the community, not an imported maid.

Juanita was born seven years after the last of the five children—an accidental pregnancy. She was given over to the care of the maid the family had brought with them from Mexico when they immigrated to the United States. Juanita was a cheery, outgoing child, spontaneous and noisy. Her father was often embarrassed by her behavior in public places, especially in restaurants. He would demand that she quiet down, then hit her in public.

He continuously told her that she was a disgrace to the family. As time went on, her brothers and sisters began to treat her with the same contempt. Only the maid remained on her side; the rest of the family called Juanita disloyal. They said she made the family look bad in public and chided her for preferring the maid over them. As a result, Juanita felt emotionally exiled from her family. She hated herself, believing her accusers.

In her junior year of high school, she cut her left wrist. She was hospitalized at a nearby psychiatric hospital for attempting suicide.

While in the hospital, she developed a pattern of head-banging in fits of anger. She would also smack the backs of her arms against the corners where two walls met—until she was given powerful tranquilizers. Juanita was on tranquilizers when she was discharged from the hospital; she stayed on them for a year.

After that year, her therapist thought it was time to taper off her medication. But within two months she began to cut herself, mostly on the wrists. She was hospitalized repeatedly for a week at a time for these so-called suicide attempts.

When Juanita entered college, she developed a pattern of excelling academically for the first three-quarters of each semester, then withdrawing to her room and not attending her final exams. She had been expelled from two colleges when she came into treatment with me.

She was likable, dressed in bright colors, and quick to explain to me that deep down she understood she was smart and a good person. She spent her first several months of therapy describing her past. When she was upset by something she had just said, she would immediately change the subject. If I asked her to return to the subject, she would tell me that it was too overwhelming for her, but that she would come back to it at a later time.

During one session, Juanita reached into her pocketbook and took out a small object. She had been speaking about one of the occasions when her father had hit her and humiliated her in a restaurant. Her mood became subdued and trancelike.

That's when she took out the pair of children's scissors, looking like a toy, with its bright green plastic handles. As she absentmindedly placed the open scissors on her forearm, I realized she intended to cut herself. I pulled her hand away and wrestled the scissors from her, flinging them on the desk behind me at the other end of the office. Juanita grabbed my arms. She was fighting me, though still in a trance state, repeating, "I need my scissors." When she finally realized that I did not have her scissors in my hands, she scanned the room and spotted them on my desk. She spent the next hour trying to get past me to the desk. It was clear that getting to cut herself was her only way of stopping the pain and anguish she was feeling. No amount of talking on my part helped. Exhausted by her efforts, she finally fell asleep in her chair.

Juanita attempted to do what most cutters avoid: she tried to cut herself in front of someone else. This was an ability she had developed during her stays at psychiatric hospitals where there is no privacy. There were other ways in which she was different from most cutters. She made very broad scars, longer than normal, and placed her cuts as high as the shoulders and chest. She detested these scars and asked a plastic surgeon to remove them. He refused after the appearance of new scars, telling her he would only deal with them once she had been cured of damaging her skin.

Juanita hated the results of her self-mutilating behavior, but she was inevitably drawn to it for the relief it brought. She would talk about her cutting episodes, but when I asked to see the scars, she was suddenly shy. She selected the largest and told me how disgusting she thought it looked. I asked to see the most recent. She rolled up her sleeve just past the elbow, and showed me the gauze pad held on with adhesive tape. She removed the tape with a sudden jerk as people do, to minimize the pain, grimacing at the pull of the material.

I commented, "You don't like all pain, then?"

She shot me a critical look. "It's never about liking pain. If I liked pain, then it wouldn't help. I hate it. That's why it helps."

"What does it feel like, then?"

"I feel terrible. I have to make my feelings go away. I use very bitter medicine to make them go away. If I'm lucky, I go away, too. When I do it, there's only the place on my skin that I'm looking at. There's nothing—no thoughts. I start to cut. It hurts. I cut a little deeper. It hurts a lot. I move the blade. It hurts much more. I start to bleed. The blood means I hurt enough to chase away all other pain. It's over. I can take a nap after I finish looking at it and cover it with a bandage."

Juanita's solution, or "bitter medicine" for her pain was indicative of her despair about the possibility that other people could be a source of support or safety for her. As the family scapegoat, she had learned to hate herself. She didn't feel entitled to succeed in school or to seek comfort from others when she was sad or upset. Like other disorders that result from failed trust relationships and attachments—eating disorders, obsessive-compulsive disorders, alcoholism, drug dependence—a behavior or a substance is used as a coping mechanism for the pain of the original wound. Self-mutilation is just the most bizarre and paradoxical example, in which pain and self-damage are used to bring about relief, safety, and security.

The self-mutilator is very sensitive to her emotional pain, but even more than that, she is despairing of the trustworthiness of others. She prefers to be the one in charge of the pain she experiences and the feeling of numbness it leaves her with.

3

WHO IS THE SELF-MUTILATOR?

I was doing a call-in radio show when someone called to find out if she was a self-mutilator. She explained that when she was about seven years old, she did many things in order to get her parents' attention and what she wanted from them. One day, all else having failed, she decided to cut herself with a kitchen knife. Her motivation, she said, was to frighten her parents, and she thought the sight of her bleeding would do that.

"I started to cut my arm and then I just yelled, 'Ouch!' because it hurt too much. I never even cut deep enough to draw blood," she said.

Clearly, this person is no self-mutilator.

How much resolution does it take to break the skin and draw blood? The nerves of the skin send pain signals to the brain to warn us of the danger from an impending injury. In the case of self-inflicted wounding, this pain acts as the body's own defense mechanism to stop one from proceeding in the effort at physical injury. If a person proceeds despite this pain, that means that he or she is motivated by something stronger than the pain, something that makes him or her capable of ignoring or enduring it.

It takes *intense feelings* to ignore pain. Think of the times you have put your foot in cold water as you entered a swimming pool, or the ocean. When you felt the cold, you may have backed out altogether, or found some easier way of getting yourself in, whether by jumping and experiencing the shock all at once, or proceeding slowly, shivering your way in. On the other hand, what if you saw a child thrashing around, perhaps about to drown? You would immediately block out, not even noticing the water temperature as you raced to save the child.

Something allows us to ignore discomfort and danger when a higher priority arises. Saving a child's life proves to be such a priority.

What priority exists for the self-mutilator, or cutter, which allows her to bypass her body's own defenses and ignore the pain? What throws this switch in the brain, and, in the absence of any necessary or noble priority, allows her to cut herself with a kitchen knife?

For the cutter, the act of creating pain (if pain is in fact experienced), or of drawing blood, is *in itself* the goal. The cutter must have experienced her own necessities, urgencies, and dangers, on an inner emotional level, that were as intense and real to her as the sight of a drowning child was to the person entering the water.

The swimmer is reacting to a real event, occurring outside him- or herself. The person in the second example is reacting to *internal* feelings—perhaps an event from the past or a collection of events, a buildup of angry or hurt feelings, or any combination of the above.

The swimmer may be saving the life of a child. He or she has a clear goal that dictates the reason for ignoring the cold water. The self-injurer may not even be aware of what she is doing to herself;

and as for reasons, these most likely elude her as well. However, she does have her own goal—an urgent and immediate one.

So, what is this goal? Her act solves no tactical problem for herself or for others, therefore we understand that she must be reacting to feelings within herself. By physically injuring herself, she is redressing existing grievances or pain **symptomatically**. This concept might strike us as ludicrous, treating one type of pain with another, but that is exactly what she is doing; that *is* her goal.

The option that she is not embracing—the one that is much more familiar to most of us—would be to take real verbal action and begin to bring her pain outside herself, where it could be diffused, shared, examined. Confronting an injustice usually relieves the tension that has built up inside. It is the way to achieve understanding. In the symptomatic or "substitute" method, the cutting never really puts the feelings of being hurt to rest, but rather provides only short-term relief. Thus, taking this route leads not only to a buildup of bad feelings, but also to an addiction to the method itself for the short-term relief it provides.

The self-injurer turns increasingly inward, away from others, abandoning any real emotional connection. This "inward turning" is bound to reduce the sense of relating to others, or **interpersonal reality**, and eventually reduces the accurate sense of reality in general. This we call **psychopathology** or mental illness. Which brings us to the question, "Why does this happen to some people and not to others?"

The Nature-Nurture Debate

Whenever mental or emotional illness is discussed, the issue of nature versus nurture comes up. Is a child born with the predisposition to any particular form of mental illness, or is that illness developed by members of the family, the community, or society? With most disorders, we can agree that the answer involves a combination of both genetic and environmental factors. (The most significant exception to this very basic statement would be the diseases that stem from organic neurological pathology, such as schizophrenia, Tourette's Syndrome, autism, and others.) Both a family's history and a patient's individual history can give us clues as to how much of a part genetics and chemistry play in the patient's disorder.

To begin with, the self-injurer is someone in whom a combination of depressive disorder and anxiety disorder are chemically present to varying degrees that are hereditary. It is important to emphasize that the levels at which these components are present in the self-mutilator range from "near normal" (very mild) all the way to "malignant" (incurable).

The presence of these genetic or chemical disorders may become apparent at significant developmental junctures, such as birth, puberty, adolescence, or departure from the family household, although the manifestation can also occur at any time in between or after these particular crossroads. The fact that a child possesses a genetic predisposition toward certain types of behavior, however, does not sentence him or her to any particular psychological or psychiatric disorder.

The form that such a chemical or otherwise genetically inherited trait ultimately takes is in large part dependent upon the child's upbringing—how he or she is nurtured. Troubled childhood or adolescent behavior can be dealt with in a variety of ways. The result can either be mild problems relating to depression and/or anxiety, or full-blown, complex disorders such as phobias, eating disorders, obsessive-compulsive disorders, borderline personality disorders, and self-mutilation.

The child who is dealt with skillfully and lovingly will not end up with one or more of the above disorders, but will have to cope with bouts of anxiety and/or depression to varying degrees. These disorders can be worked through with such solutions as psychotherapy, therapeutic support for family change, and medications. The severity as well as the type of the disorder decides which options are most helpful and appropriate.

On the other hand, if the behaviors or moods caused by these hereditary/chemical disorders are condemned, blamed on the child, or cause the parents to dislike, fear, alienate, or detach emotionally from that child, then the child is left alone. A child who has to cope with inexplicable and difficult feelings on his or her own turns inward. He or she invents safety mechanisms to escape the pain not only of the hereditary/chemical disorder itself but of being alone in this battle against the unexplained and the very scary feelings it causes. The longer this isolation of the child continues, the less likely it becomes that he or she will be treatable. The safety mechanisms that the child creates become stronger and more deeply ingrained with time, and eventually they will become a necessary part of the person. This is one way in which a full-blown personality disorder can develop.

Why Self-Mutilating?

Self-mutilators have many different reasons for their actions and are tormented by a spectrum of different feelings. Yet I consistently encounter two characteristics in all self-mutilators:

1. A feeling of mental disintegration, of inability to think.
2. A rage that can't be expressed, or even consciously perceived, toward a powerful figure (or figures) in their life, usually a parent.

For the self-mutilator, the experience of one or both of these feelings is unbearable and must therefore be "drowned out," as they report, by some immediate method. Physical pain and the sight of oneself bleeding become solutions because of their ability to overpower the strength of these feelings.

An Attempted Solution to Emotional Pain

Usually, the first incident begins with strong feelings of anger, anxiety, or panic. If the feeling is not too intense, throwing an object, or breaking or knocking something over, may settle the person down. It's when the person becomes so overwhelmed that none of these "remedies" help that we may see them plunge a fist into a wall or through a window, bang their head against a wall, or finally take a weapon to use against themselves.

Someone who stumbles upon self-injury in this manner and discovers that it relieves one of the painful states listed above will be inclined to use this discovery again in the future. The individual who needs this kind of solution is a person who cannot redress the grievances she has with others, who is afraid to argue, to articulate what she is so angry about. The self-mutilator is ashamed of the mental pain that she experiences and has no language with which to describe it to others.

However they came to it, the self-mutilator is someone who has found that physical pain can be a cure for emotional pain. It is someone who, for one reason for another, has absolutely no outlet for her emotional pain, and therefore no relief from it. All she has is that short period of time when it is temporarily overpowered, "drowned out," by physical pain.

When a person attacks his or her own body with an instrument that will wound the skin, and often worse, it means that the person feels helpless to use any other means to manage the mental anguish and chaos that is borne out of unmanageable feelings. This goes far beyond frustration. Self-mutilating behavior means the mind has slipped away from its ordinary context or perspective, losing sight of the impracticality of pain and danger in order to commit an act that will bring an immediate solution (however unrealistic or temporary in nature) to emotional pain.

Characteristics of the Self-Injurer

The person who chooses this action is someone who experiences herself as powerless. She may not be docile, timid, or shy in public; she may even be quite outgoing. But no matter how outgoing or confident she seems, she feels alone wherever she is, different from everyone around her, an outsider. She is often plagued by a fear of punishment—usually from a parent—for being deficient, inadequate, a disappointment in a way that was either specifically defined for her, or one that is unspoken but understood.

Like the anorexic, she may feel that she has no one to depend upon or to trust with her emotions. That feeling alone will produce fearfulness most of the time, even when there is no immediate cause to fear. So, what we know about this person is that she is afraid, and she may hide behind obsessional thinking or eating disorders as well as self-mutilation to gain relief from her constant state of fear. She is seeking all the relief she can find from her fearfulness. Often, she is a high achiever in some area, whether it is academics, the arts, or athletics. At the same time, she may ignore (and usually does) subjects that don't interest her. Her school record may fluctuate drastically from A's to F's.

She is often apologetic even when she has done nothing to apologize for. She is fearful of what she sees as the imminent danger or resentment others will feel toward her. Sometimes, her frequent gratuitous apologies stemming from this fear will annoy and alienate those friends closest to her. She may interpret their withdrawal as an indication that she has been offensive or not apologetic enough and increase the very behavior that repels those around her. Still, she is a person generally liked by her peer group, who may identify on a very small scale with her vulnerability, a vulnerability that most of them are also experiencing to a lesser degree.

The self-mutilator is therefore a likable, sometimes high-achieving person with a myriad of problems.

The feelings of fear and loneliness from having no one to depend upon or trust are not formed in the imagination of the self-mutilator, but usually in actual childhood or early adolescent experience. They are realistic fears, based on real experiences. There is an impressive correlation between traumatic experiences and the severity of the resulting self-mutilating behavior. Some of the trauma is subtle and may include having a parent with a mental or physical illness; being overlooked and neglected; having the family broken up or separated for a period of time. Some of the trauma is very unsubtle: physical abuse, sexual molestation, and incest rape.

Parental Behaviors That Influence Self-Mutilation

Parental aggression toward the "troubled" child will cause the child to be simultaneously protective of and afraid of displeasing her parents. This is a form of child abuse that can range from moderate to severe—one that leaves a child first with no one to blame, and then with no one to retaliate against, except herself. Usually, the self-blame builds up for years before the self-retaliation (in this case, self-mutilation) begins.

Healthy parenting does not produce a self-mutilating child. Parenting has its greatest effect on a child during the formative years of her personality development (birth to six years of age). Although these are the years when a child needs the most from her parents, it may also be a very strenuous time with regards to finances, marital relations, and the experience of each parent as he or she establishes parental identity. Establishing our identity as a parent changes the way we feel about ourselves, and is an often underestimated factor that affects the parenting process profoundly.

Two key features of a healthy parent's identity are

1. *Confidence/Authoritativeness:* Gives the child a sense of being protected from his or her own impulses as well as from the dangers of the outside world.
2. *Nurturance/Warmth:* Creates a sense of value and self-esteem in the child.

If parents themselves require support from the child, or the parents have an inadequate amount of warmth and attentiveness to offer the child, the child does not enjoy the security to express the natural negative feelings that all children occasionally experience toward their parents. The child believes that such feelings would harm her parents and leave her parentless.

If a child experiences this reversal of dependence during her formative years, she can only dare to feel anger toward herself, never toward others. She is the child who may become one form of self-mutilator, known as **nondissociative**, who suffers from intolerable rage with which she is only capable of attacking herself.

The child who, during her formative years, experiences a lack of warmth and nurturance, or who is the object of her parents' cruelty, will be the second kind of self-mutilator, the **dissociative**, who feels disconnected from her parents, from others, and ultimately from herself.★ When she experiences an "attack" of this sense of disconnection, she feels mental disintegration developing. At this point she needs a powerful distraction around which to organize and stop the mental disintegration. Pain, and her own blood, provides a sufficient distraction, and works as a tool to help the cutter center herself.

During the first six years of life, the blueprint is forming. The design usually won't make itself apparent until just prior to puberty, about ten or eleven years of age. What we see by then in a self-mutilator is a girl whose relationships have failed. Because she

★The distinctions between these two categories are explained further in chapter 8.

has not had successful emotional relationships, she has not had the opportunity to acquire the language of emotional expression we learn when we have to relate to other people. Lacking the words with which to express her emotional pain, she resorts to a destructive physical dialogue with herself.

Feelings—The Danger Zone

The self-mutilator is not someone who is articulate about her feelings. I find that many of these girls are awkward when it comes to explaining their thoughts and feelings about themselves and the relationships they have with others. They are usually unable to estimate the reactions that others will have to their words and deeds. They are, in fact, puzzled by past reactions others have had to them, and repeat their misinterpretations in everyday relations.

In other words, most self-mutilators suffer from a lack of emotional perceptiveness toward other people. In some cases, the girl is altogether unaware of the existence of the emotional life of an important other. In other cases, she has her own ideas about the feelings of those around her, but they are highly distorted ideas that do not at all resemble the emotional reality of the situation. This sometimes lacking and sometimes distorted perception of others' emotions comes from an insecurity within the self. The self-mutilator has very little physical and emotional security about herself. She lacks a foundation of understanding about herself and therefore has no consistent vantage point from which to step back and evaluate the feelings of those around her.

To sum up, in the population of self-mutilators we see a group of mostly young people who are often emotionally inarticulate and emotionally imperceptive. The lack of emotional security, as well as a real inability to express themselves emotionally with the use of language (rather than by acting out), leaves them in an emotional isolation, where life is lived at the defensive, survival level. Sonia, whose case begins below, is an example of a young woman who turned to self-mutilating to "solve" her emotional dilemma. Her case is also an example of **underparenting**: parents who did not exhibit the two features necessary to positive parenting—confidence/authority and nurturance/warmth—predisposed Sonia to self-harming behaviors.

Sonia: Coping by Cutting

Seventeen-year-old Sonia is the daughter of Cuban immigrants. She came to the United States with her family sixteen years ago, when she was one year old. The family moved to a college town in the Midwest where her father had accepted a job as an acting teacher after a long and prominent career in Cuban theater.

Sonia spoke very little Spanish, although she understood it. The midwestern community they moved to had almost no Spanish-speaking population. A major fear of Sonia's parents was that she would become Americanized. They came from an old, wealthy, conservative Cuban family, and were determined that Sonia would be a classical musician and not an actress because, in their opinion, Americans in the theater were too liberal sexually.

Sonia sat down in the overstuffed chair in my office, smiled, and maintained her smile, but said nothing. I broke the silence by asking, "Do you know why your mother made an appointment for you to see me?"

"Because I cut myself."

"Did you cut yourself once, or have you cut yourself often?"

She giggled at my question, but then seemed to fade away from the office into a daydream.

"Sonia?" I called out to get her attention.

She shook her head as if trying to dispel the trance. Her eyes darted around the room, rarely meeting mine.

"Sonia," I repeated, "what do you do to hurt yourself?"

"I don't know—it's different all the time."

I was jumping the gun. I realized that cataloguing her symptomatic behaviors was premature and useless to treatment and re-covery until this very isolated girl formed a connection with me. At this point I couldn't even stay in her focus for more than sec-onds at a time, much less begin to form a relationship we could use to rid her of her symptoms.

I moved my chair a bit closer, in hopes that it would make it more difficult for her to "drift" or go into a dissociative state. She looked rather surprised, almost frightened at the shift.

"You look worried or frightened that I moved my chair closer to you. Are you afraid that I will harm you?"

"Well," she said, and paused to think before continuing, "I guess—not *you.*"

"You mean others have hurt you?"

"Sure. Doesn't that happen to everyone?"

"It depends on what kind of hurting we are talking about, and who is doing it and how often. Do your parents hurt you?"

"Sure. Don't everybody's?"

"I think that most children have experienced their parents' being angry at them, losing their temper at them, even spanking them. However, it's usually rare and does not cause damage to the child in the form of scratches, bruises, cuts, burns, or broken bones. When these kinds of injuries result, we call it child abuse."

She stared at me, almost in disbelief. I had put her own experi-ences, that she had never described to anyone, into words. She did not "slip away" while I had been speaking. I continued:

"In the first example I gave you, which is not child abuse, the relationship between parent and child is, for the most part, kind, loving, caring, and protective on the parent's part, and there is a bond between parent and child which includes talk and commu-nication."

I still hadn't lost her, but after the second explanation, she was beginning to slip away again. I had put her in conflict with what was possibly a young lifetime of accepting abuse. It was becoming clear that she handled conflict by "zoning out" or cutting herself when she was unable to tune out her painful experiences. For Sonia, avoiding conflict was her top emotional priority. Conflict could cause her to act out toward her parents in a way she feared, because as she told me in a later session, it would cause them to hurt her, stop loving her, or protest to her that she was "killing them."

These protests by her parents about how they suffered at the hands of her "misbehavior" (normal teenage behavior that included coming home from school a little late or failing to practice her cello enough) had at least as powerful an effect on her as their beatings. This emotional abuse rivaled the physical abuse Sonia endured, such as her mother scratching her bow arm, or slapping her in the face as hard as she could.

Sonia internalized all of her punishments and experienced them as feelings of abandonment and rejection, which made her believe that she was alone and uncared for in this world. Since she couldn't depend on her parents (or anyone else), she was left feeling that the only thing she could do was try to "control" her painful feelings of abandonment.

When I spoke of abuse, it dredged up Sonia's most terrible and terrifying feelings of loneliness and abandonment, her memories of physical and emotional pain. In order to control the impact these feelings had on her in her young lifetime, Sonia had learned how to escape—by zoning out. It was apparent that this trance state Sonia went into, when first I asked her about the frequency of her self-injury and then again when I spoke of child abuse, was neither a new nor a rare experience for her. It was a defense she had created and used (often enough for it to be brought to the attention of her parents) in order to protect herself from painful and confusing feelings. She was now enlisting her number one defense against my attempts to get her to talk about the feelings from which that defense had always shielded her.

I watched her fade out in front of me and decided not to interfere. I was hoping that somewhere in her awareness, she would realize that I was not going to be angry, or punish her for "misbehaving" toward me by zoning out during our session.

I allowed three minutes of silence and then said, "I think you needed to leave me for a while because what I said to you was too hard to hear." She kept spacing out. I realized that since she had put herself into a sort of trance, I had forgotten my hypnosis training and hadn't addressed her by name, requesting that she come out of the trance.

"Sonia," I requested firmly, "I would like you to come out of your trance."

She focused her eyes, shook her head a bit, and smiled in appeasement at me.

I repeated what I had said to her before, and added almost apologetically, "I guess by saying that when your parents hurt you it is not an okay thing but rather child abuse, I said some welcome but very scary things to you." I kept up a strong but sympathetic eye contact with her.

"Once, my father smashed my cello to bits when I put it down after I had stopped practicing five minutes early." Her appeasing smile had disappeared.

I was pleased at having bridged the emotional chasm between Sonia and the rest of her world, but I realized that this bridge was fragile and would have to be rebuilt many times. I sat silently as she continued:

"If I made too many mistakes, my mother would grab my bow arm and dig her nails into it. Sometimes my arm bled."

She spaced out again.

"Sonia? . . . Sonia, did that hurt?"

She shrugged her shoulders, still staring straight ahead. She wasn't completely withdrawing into her trance state. "It would hurt most people. They might cry."

One tear slid from her left eye. Her trance deepened. After three silent minutes had passed, I spoke in a loud, almost strident tone. "Sonia, we must make other appointments. Today we have to make our next appointment."

She came halfway out. It seemed she knew that I was talking to her but wasn't sure what I had said.

"Sonia. Appointment time."

"Huh? What do you mean?"

"We have to make our next appointment."

"Oh." (Still dazed) "Okay."

"What time do you finish school?"

"Two-thirty," she responded promptly, sounding more alert. "But I have cello lessons after that."

"What days do you have lessons?"

"Mondays and Thursdays."

"Can you come on Tuesdays?"

"I think so." She was completely alert now. "Yes, Tuesdays will be fine."

"I would like to meet with your parents."

She looked alarmed. "Why?"

"To see what they're like."

"They'll be mad at me! And my father's out of town. The theater group travels a lot."

"Why would they be mad at you? They sent you here."

"Because of what I told you."

"I don't tell your parents what you say here."

She looked relieved but not completely comfortable.

"In the future you will probably say a lot of things you don't want anyone ever to hear. You'll be able to say those kinds of things *because* no one else will ever hear them. This is your private thinking and talking place . . . You'll see."

Sonia's mother came in two days later. She wore a conservative suit with a small turquoise silk scarf, indicating a bit of discreet flair. She had dark hair pulled back in a bun, and gold hoop earrings. Her eyes were large and almost black, deepset, the eyebrows

poised down toward the bridge of her nose. She could be impos-
ing and intimidating at will. Today, she was a worried mother, but
I had been subtly warned.

"I don't understand why a person, no less my daughter, would
want to hurt herself, cause herself pain, and scar her beautiful skin.
Is she some kind of crazy?"

Somehow her Cuban accent helped her get to the point very
quickly. I thought I would use her simplified idiom to my advantage.

"Yes. She is crazy when she does this behavior."

"Is she crazy all the time? She goes to school, practices cello. I
don't get complaints from the school that she acts crazy there."

"No. I don't think she is crazy all the time, but the times she be-
haves this way could become more frequent, as well as cause damage to her physically."

"You mean that she could become like a cripple? Then she
wouldn't be able to play the cello, or have a normal life."

"How does she behave at home? Is she moody, angry, sad,
cheerful?"

"I don't think she is moody most of the time. Sometimes she
looks sad. When I ask her what's wrong, she always says, 'Nothing.'
Most of the time she has no expression on her face, except when
she is playing the cello, then she has a look of fierce determination. When she puts it down, she becomes blank again."

"How does she get along with you and your husband?"

She looked angry now. "My husband travels so much with the
college acting group, when he's not rehearsing until all hours. He
hardly sees her. It's like I'm bringing her up myself. I get along
with her real well. We don't fight or argue. Sometimes her room
is messy." She donned a charming, almost mischievous smile. "But
maybe you have teenagers? That's normal, not crazy. No?"

"No, messy is definitely not crazy. I do think that I will have to
see her once a week to prevent this from getting worse, and hopefully make it go away."

"Of course. I hear wonderful things about you. I'm sure you can do this job successfully. Would you like me to come back? Can I call you if I'm worried about her getting out of control with this? I don't want her to cripple or kill herself."

"Yes, of course. We just can't discuss what she says here."

She made a slight frown, followed by a knowing smile. "Of course not. I would not want to hear what she says or any of the terrible things you must hear from the other people you see."

Sonia's father came in the following week: a handsome man at forty-five (three years older than his wife), dressed in bluejeans and a black turtleneck.

"I'm glad and relieved to meet you," he began. "I wanted Sonia to go into music almost for safety. A lot of the kids I work with have so many problems and so few plans for their futures. They don't understand how competitive it is out there. They think Hollywood and Broadway are just waiting for them. Sonia causes me great pain. That she does these things to herself breaks my heart. I think maybe it hurts me even more than it does her. Sometimes I am in so much pain that when I'm home I pay little attention to her, to let her know I'm disappointed with this behavior. When she can tell me it's over, I'll be closer with her. I am a director; people listen to me all day long. In my own home I can't even direct my daughter to stop damaging herself. I think a child is more draining than directing a whole troupe of actors—even under Castro."

He did not ask any questions about his daughter, her pathological behavior, the prognosis, what he should do to help her.

"Well, I hope *you* can direct her out of this dangerous behavior." He looked at his watch. "I'm sorry to cut this short but I have a rehearsal to go to."

He shook my hand briefly and left.

Sonia came in for her second appointment. She looked suspicious and worried. "They liked you. Did *you* like them?"

"Do you want me to like them?"

She shrugged. "I don't care. As long as they like you, they won't be mad if I come here, although my father already made a remark about how expensive it is for me to see you and that I better stop this behavior because of the sacrifices he is making so I can see you.

"My mother liked you. I think she likes you better than she likes my father. Is that right?"

"I guess they don't get along so well with each other."

"I think that they hate each other, but I don't care."

"I don't think that I need to meet with them again."

Sonia seemed relieved. All the worries she had implied appeared to vanish. She looked at me directly. "You know she doesn't hit me or scratch me anymore. *He* always is either cold to me or busy feeling sorry for himself. At least he can't damage my cello again." She smiled with satisfaction.

"Why not?"

"I'm not on scholarship at my fancy private school just because some foolish people think I'm good. The cello I play has been lent to me by a collector. It's worth over a hundred thousand dollars. I'm not sure how much."

Sonia, now reassured that I wasn't an agent of her parents' motives, was talking in slightly longer sentences with less difficulty. She had begun to enter into a treatment relationship with me.

Sonia is an example of a victim of parental loss of temper, narcissistic self-pity, and cruelty. She is not at the extreme end of the spectrum, which includes girls who are the victims of sexual abuse and incest. Nevertheless, she shows many of the symptoms of those victims. She is conversationally shy, and avoids anything resembling closeness, or self-disclosure. She uses pain and blood to release her feelings of abandonment, anger, and despair. In this way she avoids a state of mental disintegration—the inner bombardment by chaotic thoughts that seem disconnected to each other.

The self-mutilator is typically a young woman who has not formed healthy attachments with parental figures. By physically injuring herself, she is making an attempt to redress the pain she was accustomed to as a young child. What she fails to realize is that by harming herself, she never really confronts the feelings of being hurt or neglected. Self-injury provides only short-term relief.

The account of Sonia's treatment continues in Part Two, as we explore the complex processes of change and recovery.

4

THE REACTIONS OF OTHERS

The Public

Recently, I was a guest on another talk show (this time on television) about self-mutilation. The host was highly experienced at her job, but when we got into the ways that self-mutilators harm themselves, her upper lip began to twitch and she started to characterize their behavior in strong words, including "grotesque." I interrupted her by speaking directly to the camera:

"Most of you watch emergency-room medicine and open-heart surgery on television while eating dinner or sitting on the couch. Here we are for the most part talking about minor cuts, lacerations, and burns that many of you have experienced without getting very upset. Some of you have had to apply ordinary first aid to your own children when they hurt themselves. Perhaps what makes this concept of self-harming so difficult to cope with is the feeling that the person doing this to him- or herself is suffering from some dreadful madness that may accelerate until they damage themselves terribly."

My point was to bring the issue back into perspective. I believe that the public's fantasies do, in fact, run to extremes and that the mildest word most of us can use to describe self-mutilating behavior is "disgusting." In order to help these disturbed individuals, we must first understand and overcome the origins of our own disgust.

When I was treating severe anorexics in the 1970s in urban teaching hospitals, I discovered that the staff was very angry at them. Both doctors and nurses were annoyed that they had to waste their time on patients who were starving themselves to malnutrition when they had plenty to eat. The anorexics were deliberately causing themselves harm and wasting valuable hospital beds that people with serious and involuntary medical problems could be using. These patients were uncooperative and self-sabotaging. They were also sabotaging the help their doctors were trying to administer.

Professionals in mental health, patients' families, and the general public all harbor a very similar attitude toward the self-mutilator as their counterparts had to the emaciated anorexic about twenty years ago. The self-mutilator is looked upon with fear, anger, disgust, and revulsion.

In the case of the eating disorders, anorexia and bulimia, a younger group of mental health professionals emerged, determined to understand the illnesses, their causes, and the specifics of the behaviors involved. This population of clinicians learned how to desensitize themselves to the unusual and unattractive behaviors of their patients, and to the equally unattractive physical results of these behaviors.

Twenty years later, we are at that same sort of pivotal point in clinical history, where the same changes must happen in the mental health field for the self-mutilating patient. Desensitizing ourselves to the behaviors and the scars they inflict does not mean desensitizing ourselves to the patient's emotional distress. It is, rather, the first step necessary to seeing the self-mutilator for what she is—a person in desperate need of help and human contact.

The Family

When family members find out that a child is cutting, burning, or in some other way harming herself, their first reaction is fright. This reaction often evolves into rage: "How can you be so stupid or crazy to do this to yourself?" No parent easily accepts that their son or daughter is showing signs of mental illness. It is easier for them to rationalize that the child will outgrow this behavior. Common parental responses include assuming that it is merely brattiness, stubbornness, just a phase. Loved ones may also be too shocked to see past their own hurt feelings. Many parents respond narcisstically: "You are trying to upset me or make me feel guilty by sabotaging all my good parenting and the love I have shown you. How ungrateful of you!"

The Professionals

Recently, a young woman of twenty-four was referred to me. At the initial interview she reported, "The first two therapists I saw told me they couldn't help me because they were not familiar with self-mutilation."

"How did that make you feel about yourself?" I asked her.

"Like I was a freak—beyond their comprehension to understand—or that maybe they were afraid of what was wrong with me. It also made me feel that I was hopeless."

Was it possible that the therapists were, like the general public, repelled by her behavior, frightened by physical damage she inflicted upon herself? Might they have even been afraid of their liability should serious harm or death result from a treatment failure? Of course, we will never know for sure. What we do know is that when a patient is rejected for psychotherapy, he or she feels wounded and perhaps untreatable. On the other hand, when a therapist realizes that he or she cannot competently treat someone who is seeking help, it is highly ethical to indicate this, rather than attempt a treatment with which the therapist is unfamiliar.

In contrast to the mystery that self-mutilation currently poses to the mental health profession, we will soon be seeing a trend toward familiarization with the illness. I envisage that a few years hence there will be self-help groups and specialized treatment centers for those who harm themselves, just as there are now for the eating-disordered, drug addicts, alcoholics, compulsive gamblers, and other groups seeking professional and peer support.

The Media

Television, radio, women's service magazines, and newspapers initially presented self-mutilators as freaks. This is simply the way a nation's attention is attracted to a problem of this nature. As negative as it is, even this introductory period can be helpful in its capacity to demystify an unfamiliar sickness. The quicker the introduction, the better for the victims.

If the media echoes the same message that ambivalent parents, out of love for their children, are sending—"I'm afraid of your illness"—then we have done a disservice to the victim who dares to come out with her terrible secret.

In fortunate cases, the family of a patient is willing and able to provide her with as much emotional support as she needs to become healthy. Friends, however, may not be able to generate an inexhaustible amount of caring. They may recoil in fear, or go to the other extreme and try single-handedly to rescue their friend from this self-destructive behavior. If they abandon the sufferer, her illness may deepen. If they attempt to save or rescue her and fail, they may turn away because she would then be a symbol of their own failure. In both scenarios the self-mutilator ends up abandoned.

Real information about the disorder, not drama, is the surest way to stabilize the patient's reaction. Whether we are family, friend, or therapist, we need to convey to the victims that we understand that they are resorting to an unhealthy behavior in order to relieve psychological pain. We must reinforce for the sufferer that the self-mutilating behavior is only a small part of who they are, not the whole picture.

Many self-help organizations for substance addictions, eating disorders, and other problems inadvertently assist the victim in the creation of a false identity. The members of these groups come to perceive themselves as existing solely in terms of the disorder they are trying to get rid of. They accept the message that "You will always be . . . an alcoholic, drug addict, etc." There goes that pendulum out of control again. While we want to stress the importance of overcoming disordered and self-destructive behavior, we also want to stress that someday this will be in the past. In order to help the self-mutilator, we have to credit her with a more rounded identity. We cannot simply see her as one-dimensional— a person who harms herself. *A victim's illness is not her identity.*

Mildred: A Mask of Glibness

When Mildred came into my office, she proudly introduced herself by saying: "I have an eating disorder, am obsessive-compulsive, and have been cutting and sometimes burning myself for the last three years. The first two problems go back at least five or six years. I've seen five psychiatrists, been in three psych hospitals, and belong to three self-help groups."

I responded: "It sounds like your life has been taken over by these problems. Do you have any personal features other than your illnesses?"

Mildred was crestfallen. "You don't appreciate the seriousness of my problems. Perhaps I should see someone else who will."

"I'm concerned that you have somehow gotten lost amid the psychiatric problems you've got and have lost track of who you *are*. If you want to find out who that is, I would be delighted to work with you on that issue while we are also working on your identified diagnoses."

Mildred entered treatment.

Mildred's opening statement was presented far more glibly than was appropriate for the gravity of its content. This was a clear indication to me that she was very uncomfortable receiving help from someone else, especially when the project with which she needed help was herself.

"You don't want to be here, do you?" I asked her.

She looked surprised. "What do you mean?"

"My guess is that you are more comfortable with the roles of caretaker, supporter, shoulder-to-cry-on, than being the person in need herself. In this therapy you are the recipient of care, not the giver of care. I think that you don't know how to do that."

"Well, I don't know. We just met. How could I trust you to be a caregiver to me?"

"You are right, of course. But let me ask you just who do you accept emotional care from when you're feeling needy?"

"I don't know what you mean."

"Who do you cry to?"

"Sometimes my friends."

"Can you lean on your friends?"

"I'm not sure."

"What do you imagine would happen if you were needy with your friends?"

She paused, frowned, and fixed her eyes on the rug as she spoke. "I think that they wouldn't like me anymore. They might even get mad at me. And I would hate myself."

"That must make you feel lonely and separate."

"Why?"

"If no one knows who you are, bad moods included, then you must feel alone with your sadness. There are probably lots of parts of your personality that you can't show others because you fear that reaction you just told me about."

She shrugged tearfully.

"I am going to help you show me those parts of your personality that you can't show your friends."

"How can you do that?"

"I think what you're asking is, 'What can one person do for another?' The answer to that question is, 'Much more than you think.' "

At that, Mildred looked stunned. I asked her to explain the expression on her face.

She responded incredulously, "How can you say that to someone you just met? How can you even know that? I might turn out to be someone you can't . . . I might even be too much for you! I'm too much for my parents, and I've been too much for the last three therapists who tried to help me, if you can call it that."

"If you have so many doubts about whether or not I can help you," I replied, "why do you look so scared? Are you afraid to hope?" At this she became a little teary. "Is there a little Mildred inside of you who wishes to hope? Do you have to tell her to shut up when she does?"

Mildred began to sob openly.

"I guess I was just talking to little Mildred, that part of you that wants to hope. I guess that's who's behind that mask of glibness you came in here wearing. Aren't you glad you took that mask off?"

"It's scary without the mask. I don't know who's there and I don't know what will happen to her."

"Then you need a guide to show you who's there."

"Why should I trust you?" she asked, still sobbing.

"You already trust me a little, and that's a lot for our first meeting. I think that you will trust me more than that blade and the pain it brings you."

She shook her head in defiance.

"We will make this a gradual exchange," I assured her. "I'm not in a hurry. The development of trust can't be hurried. I guess I'm asking you not to rush yourself. That may strike you as strange, but I'm thinking long term."

"I still might turn out to be too much for you, you know. The sword cuts both ways. You just met me and you've already decided you think you can help me."

I smiled. "I think you are too much for *you.*"

"We'll just have to wait and see." She broke into a friendly smile and wiped her eyes.

"So I guess you're coming back for more of this?"

"Yeah, yeah. I guess you better get your appointment book out and see when you can fit me in."

"When you really get moving, we'll see about two meetings a week."

"Oh great! You want to see how much I can take, huh?"

"No. I think *you* want to see how much you can take."

Mildred had indicated that she was reachable nearly from the moment she came into the room. The thin veneer of bravado was an easy barrier to break through. Self-mutilators, like anorexics, have bizarre, mystifying, and dangerous behaviors to mask their fears and keep others frightened of getting too close. The distance they learn to establish arises from their hopelessness, and keeps the value of their symptoms intact. *The easiest way to break through this defense is to indicate that you are comfortable getting close to the person's pain, rage, and despair.* Kindly and comfortably devaluing the symptoms that have intimidated others is a rapid route to developing a trusting relationship with such a patient. This is one of the first but, sadly, not the last obstacles to treatment.

Mildred was not as entrenched in her self-mutilating symptoms as her glib but dazzling inventory of her pathological behaviors might have implied. There was an underlying health within her.

Breaking Down the Barriers

It is always difficult to isolate why one person develops severe psychopathology and another does not. Even when all the family relationship factors and histories of mental health or illness are tallied, one sibling does well while another does poorly. We have to keep in mind that behavioral symptoms for any illness serve as the tip of the iceberg: they could indicate profound disturbance and a poor prognosis, or simply be the proverbial "cry for help" that, when dealt with promptly and skillfully, resolves the underlying problems.

Merely knowing that someone is a self-mutilator, or an anorexic, is not enough. We need to build a developmental history that will tell us, diagnostically, of any underlying personality, mood, anxiety, or neurological disorders that could affect the outcome of treatment, as well as determining how intense that treatment should be.

If Mildred, for all her symptoms, was on the less profoundly disturbed end of the continuum, Dina was at the opposite end. Dina is an example of a self-mutilator who has created a false identity for herself.

Dina: A Mask of Friendliness

Dina came into her first session with a smile on her face. She was friendly, likable, and outgoing. She had been referred to me by a local psychiatric hospital where she had spent three weeks as a consequence of a suicide attempt. The director phoned to warn me that although Dina could be endearing, she was unpredictable and could get into severe trouble with surprising swiftness. With Dina's approval, the file was mailed to me by the hospital. It indicated a history of hospitalizations and emergency-room visits going back five years, since Dina had turned fifteen. The emergency-room visits led to short, two- to three-day stays in the hospital for observation. They were brought on by either an overdose of a hodgepodge of medications, or a severe self-inflicted wound (usually done with a dull instrument that would make a cut broad enough to require stitches).

Nothing about her initial session suggested that Dina could be severely disturbed. There were no outward signs to suggest that she was a danger to herself and had already been in treatment with five therapists for varying lengths of time with little or no improvement in her mood changes, her lack of self-esteem, or her self-destructive symptoms.

Dina did not attempt to conceal her history, but her way of telling it suggested that most of her problems were in the past and that she was making lots of progress in getting rid of her remaining problems.

After she had reassured me of her vast improvement, I asked her if I might see some of the scars she had "from the past."

"Oh sure, but be prepared. They are ugly. I'm thinking of having some of them removed by a plastic surgeon."

With that she pulled up her short sleeve, uncovered her shoulder, and revealed a scar an eighth of an inch wide and three inches long.

"Did you cut a tendon or any nerves when you did that?"

She was disappointed at my lack of shock but pleased that I knew how serious her cutting was.

"No, but the doctor said that I barely missed badly damaging my shoulder joint. I don't care about that, but I just hate how ugly it looks now. The pinkness won't even fade like the others. It's been a year. I took a bunch of pills, drank some vodka, and made the cut with a serrated knife."

"I imagine that you took the pills and the vodka to kill the pain?"

"No, I took them to make sure that I would do it."

Her facial expression changed swiftly to seething anger and determination. It was one of those "changes" the director of the psychiatric hospital had warned me about. I sat there in silence for a minute. She caught herself and donned her engaging smile again. "Well, anyway, that's all over with."

"But it seemed to me like you just relived those old feelings for a few minutes there."

"Yeah, I guess they—the feelings—still come and go now and then." She looked and sounded more resigned now.

"Are you at a point where you believe that you'll never act on them again?"

"I keep thinking that I'm at that point, but just when I begin to believe it, I do it again."

"Cut yourself?"

"Cut myself, starve myself, throw up, spend the day cleaning my room over and over, rearranging everything obsessively until it's time to go to sleep. Sometimes I think that I'll always be crazy."

"I guess you're pretty used to all this by now?"

"I'm used to it and I hate it."

In Dina's case, we see a pattern of self-mutilation that deepened until it became truly dangerous to her. By the time of our first session, Dina's disorder had reached a level where she could, in a state of drug and alcohol intoxication, inadvertently cut an artery and not even be aware of what she did. Such behavior could lead to accidental suicide. This kind of deepening of the disorder was not motivated by the self-mutilation's usefulness in relieving emotional pain. Rather, it was a result of other personality and mood disorders that were destabilizing her.

In later sessions, Dina would lash out at me with her anger, which could dissipate as quickly as it had appeared. She would make plans based on two successful (symptom-free) weeks and become unable to follow up on them. These plans might involve starting a college course, or a demanding job; she would then abandon the course, and get fired from the job for excessive absence. She would ascribe her failures in these areas to recurring depressions that immobilized her, or fears of failure that caused her to back away from attending class or showing up for work.

Dina had been evaluated by several psychopharmacologists for medications and many had been tried—sometimes singly, other times in combination. Still her behavioral patterns continued and her cutting disorder deepened as she simultaneously "lost the willpower" to starve herself. It seemed that cutting was the easiest of her disorders to maintain.

Dina's prognosis was poorer than most. She embraced the identity of "mental patient" and abandoned the remainder of her high school friends, preferring the other patients she met in psychiatric hospitals. This change of peer groups made her illness feel more normal since all of her friends were grappling with similar problems. At the same time, she would become very upset when she heard that one of her friends was readmitted to a hospital due to a psychological crisis. Dina's symptoms were a reflection of the deepening of multiple disorders and the deterioration of her general mental health.

There are many ways we can react to someone with an illness. The nature of our reaction depends in large part upon how the person appears to us. As we have seen with the contrasting examples of Mildred and Dina, patients are not always what they appear to be. One who wears her pathological symptoms like badges of honor may be very reachable, while another who comes across as positive and stable may in fact be very sick. The important thing to remember is that no one is the sum of her symptoms. Behind "grotesque" behavior and "disgusting" scars there is always an individual with her own needs and her own pain.

5

HOW THE DISORDER

TAKES SHAPE

norexics occasionally cut or even burn themselves. Bulimics, and those who suffer from a combination of severe anxiety and depression, injure themselves as well. People with the diagnosis of borderline personality disorder do the same thing occasionally, or even frequently. But in all these cases, the self-injuring behavior remains secondary to the more prevalent symptoms that constitute the **primary disorder**. It remains a **feature** of the larger primary diagnosis. If we view all such disordered behaviors as a person's attempt to drive away emotional pain, then we see that self-injury is a small part of that repertoire. The method such patients rely on most to stave off emotional pain—the "method of choice"— belongs to the primary diagnosis, or disorder.

It is when a self-injuring behavior begins as one of the many symptoms and becomes promoted to most often used, to the point where all other symptoms are employed less, or with less intensity, that the person has developed a full-blown diagnosis of **self-mutilator**. This is usually a gradual process, during which other defenses accompany the increased use of self-injury. These other personality defense mechanisms include rage, frequent dissociation, and amnesia. Often, such defenses are coupled with self-hatred, or a fear of personality disintegration (the loss of the ability to think or to use cognitive abilities).

In these cases, the disordered person responds to the strong tactile stimulus of the destruction of their own skin by means of cutting, scraping (lacerating), or burning it. The self-mutilator is also responding to the intense visual stimulus that accompanies the physical damage: seeing one's own blood flowing out of the body through the skin surface. This combination of tactile and visual experiences may become the most frequently used behavior to ward off, and induce relief from, the dreaded feelings listed earlier.

Once this has happened, the use of self-mutilating behaviors can become even further amplified, to a point where they are used when the individual only anticipates or suspects that the feelings may arise in the near future. Eventually, the behavior is resorted to as an impulse, devoid of the thought processes just described, and employed as quickly and thoughtlessly as the nail-biter begins gnawing away at his or her fingernails.

Tracy: The Disorder Takes Shape

Tracy was a twenty-year-old who had first begun cutting herself at the age of fifteen. She had developed anorexia nervosa when she was fourteen and was hospitalized for three months. She was discharged at a normal weight of one hundred ten pounds for her height of five feet four inches. Her family history included being frequently beaten by her alcoholic father, who often used a strap with a sharp buckle that sometimes cut her, in addition to the welts that the leather made on her skin. Her mother never interfered with these beatings, which she often instigated herself by complaining to her husband about some misdeed Tracy had done.

Despite the beatings, Tracy respected her father and even worried about how his drinking might be harming him. He took her to football and hockey games, and they occasionally played one-on-one basketball using the hoop he had installed in the driveway when Tracy's older brother was born. Her feelings toward her dad were a mixture of worry, love, rage, and hatred. She had always been distant with her mother, who felt wounded by this. "Home" for Tracy was always a combination of the mixed feelings she had for her father along with a sense of guilt for the contemptuous feelings she expressed toward her mother.

When Tracy was fourteen, a boy called her "Thunder thighs." She didn't mention it to her parents but never forgot the insult. A year later, she began to diet. She had a fear of being stopped by her parents so she lost weight rapidly, dropping from one hundred fifteen to ninety pounds in two months. It was the school nurse who noticed the weight loss and notified her parents with a phone call.

Almost a year later, she came into my office wearing long sleeves on a warm day. I knew they were concealing a variety of cuts and scrapes; this information was in her referral. I looked straight at her and mildly asked if she would please roll up her sleeve so I could see the damage she had done to herself. She was surprised at my slow, careful examination of each cut and laceration. "Quite a variation," I commented.

"Each one depended on my mood at the time, I suppose," she replied.

"Your parents didn't notice your weight loss; how did they cope with it?"

She smiled. "My father was lost. He knew how to punish me when I did the 'wrong' thing. He didn't know how to act when he was worried. My pediatrician's warnings of the dangers of losing weight bothered my mother as well. I liked their worrying about me. After being sent home from the hospital, it seemed like it was my parents who backed away from me this time. I lost ten of the twenty pounds that the hospital put back on me. Something had changed, though. I found that I missed my old relationship with my parents, no matter how screwed up it was. I felt lonely.

"One day I found my father's largest belt, the one he would hit me with before I got sick. It was just slung over the banister at the bottom of the stairs. I picked it up and took it to my room. I sat on the edge of my bed examining the buckle carefully. It was a cowboy-style belt. The buckle was rectangular; its corners were sharp and pointed. It struck me as odd. I had felt the pain of those corners, and had seen the cuts and lacerations they left behind, but I had never wondered what the weapon looked like. Now I had control of it.

"I turned it, fingering each corner for its sharpness. I held it in my right hand and thought about how awkward it would be to cut myself on my butt as he had often done by hitting me with the belt. Besides, I wanted to see the cutting myself. So I cut my left forearm, deeper and longer than the cuts from when my dad was the one holding the belt. The more it hurt, the deeper I cut. I finally stopped at the sight of a stream of blood running from the cut down to my elbow and onto my pants.

"I stared at it for a few moments, then ran to the bathroom sink to rinse my pants and wrap some toilet paper around my arm to stop the bleeding. I used nearly half the roll, or it felt like it, anyway. My feelings of loneliness went away."

Tracy had fused attachment with pain. For the rest of us who do not have her experience, it is hard to imagine that the same pain that was dealt out to her as punishment could be used to relieve her loneliness by symbolically reestablishing a connection to her father. However, because this is a psychopathological resolution to her problem of loneliness, and not a real solution to her wish for attachment, which would involve a healthy relationship with another caring person, it is only a quick fix—a superficial relief—and an addictive one at that. That is to say, the symptom does not resolve the real problem, so it has to be repeated again and again to fend off the painful feelings that the unsolved problem continues to produce.

By the time Tracy came in for treatment, her awareness of the original reason for the self-injuring behavior was no longer enough to stop it. Yet there was still value in having that awareness because it gave Tracy a reason to trust someone else and generated a desire to diminish and eventually eliminate that behavior.

Oftentimes, the more chronic the behavior, the closer it becomes to being the disorder itself rather than a feature of the original disorder. This was the case with Tracy, whose disordered behavior began with anorexia before she had ever cut herself.

Tracy told me that after the first few times she cut herself, she took to doing so almost daily. Even on days when she was not upset, she would make little cuts. Sometimes she would choose her upper thighs (another invisible location) and designate that area for the anticipation of bad feelings. In effect, Tracy had become addicted to self-injury to ward off even the possibility of feeling any sort of emotional pain. It was her security, her medicine.

The Cycle of Separateness

The deeper Tracy got into her symptom, the further she drifted from important relationships, which threw her deeper into her symptom, and so the cycle went. A secondary problem here is that the more separate Tracy became, the more disordered she was likely to become. With no one to help form her inner reality, she would drift further and further away from any reality.

I am here referring to an aspect of emotional development that occurs first in childhood and continues throughout life. The human self, made up of our innermost thoughts and feelings, is verified when reflected back to us by a trusted person. *We are validated when we are understood.*

A major reason I approached Tracy so directly and intensely is that I had to break through the separateness Tracy had become so used to. Breaking through this wall requires certain credentials. The therapist has to be experienced as a potentially trustworthy, helpful, and competent person. His function is to form a powerful connection between security and kindness in order to replace the original fusion of pain and attachment.

The therapist will have to monitor the patient's self-mutilating behavior in the same way that someone treating a low-weight anorexic would consistently weigh her. A familiarity with each cut, burn, or bruise, and a recommendation as to how to treat it, including referring the patient to a physician or even a medical hospital, brings the therapist closer to the patient who has achieved **disorder** status (determined when self-mutilation becomes the most prevalent symptom). Here it should be noted that when the patient's behavior has amplified beyond a feature to the level of a disorder, the pacing of the therapy and the therapist's expectations for change must be extended to include a longer period of treatment.

In Tracy's case, we saw extreme parental abuse lead to the extreme: self-mutilating disorder. Other less extreme, even subtle family situations can lead to the development of self-mutilating as a feature, which is more easily treatable.

Remaining at the "Feature" Level

Self-mutilating remains at the feature level, where it is easiest to stop, when it is identified early. Usually, other psychological disorders are present and have been diagnosed. These disorders commonly include:

- Borderline personality disorder
- Eating disorders: anorexia nervosa and bulimia nervosa
- Episodes of psychotic behavior

- Severe rage, especially when it has to be concealed
- Depression coupled with anxiety
- Trichotillomania (hair-pulling)
- Obsessive-compulsive disorder

When a person is being treated for any of these illnesses, her physician should be examining her regularly for signs of self-mutilation. If any evidence is discovered, it should of course be reported to her psychotherapist.

Simone: An Anorexic Beginning

Simone, a fifteen-year-old from France, had recently moved to the United States. Her family became concerned about her refusal, or inability, to socialize in school, as well as her unhappy demeanor at home. Often retiring to her bedroom with little to say to her parents, she became mysterious to them. Her mother blamed herself for taking her daughter away from her friends in France. Simone also had difficulty with English. She was a perfectionist, and her floundering in the new language contributed to her reasons for not wanting to talk.

Simone was losing weight beyond the cosmetically acceptable, and was becoming overly fastidious about her clothing and makeup, where formerly she was quite casual about these things.

I was first consulted by her parents, who were concerned that she was becoming "out of reach," as they put it. I followed up our consultation with a call to the examining physician, who informed me that Simone was in good health generally, but if she continued to lose weight she would develop physical problems related to anorexia. I asked him if he had noticed any remarkable damage to her skin (cuts, lacerations, burns, or suspicious scarring). He responded that he had not been looking for those kinds of problems but said he would be glad to reexamine her. I requested that he do so before I saw Simone for our initial meeting.

I always weigh a patient referred for anorexia nervosa during our first meeting. However, as I am not a physician, I would not examine her for skin damage beyond what showed when she was fully dressed.

The physician reported to me that he found a number of minor scars, an inch in length, as well as a few fresh cuts, the same length, apparently made with a sharp instrument. Three of the cuts were on her upper left thigh, an example of what a cutter would consider a good hiding place for her sickness.

Simone came to my office for her first appointment in bluejeans and a long-sleeve shirt. The weather was sunny and the temperature in the mid-eighties. Simone was taking no chances. As she walked into the office, she looked as if she had come to the appointment under some sort of threat.

"Are you here because you wanted to see a therapist or were you coerced into coming?" I asked her.

"The second choice is the most true," she said, nodding her head, pleased that she could be brief and concise in English. She smiled.

"Then it will be slightly more difficult for us to do the work we have to do," I answered, as if she had in fact expressed interest in working with me to change her situation.

"What work is that?"

"The talk between us that will help you stop needing to cut yourself on your arms and legs."

I stopped there and allowed for silence. Simone became a bit tense. She stuck out her lower lip a little and looked down at the floor. She was not prepared for her most secret behavior to be revealed. She seemed to be expecting a scolding for this behavior. In addition, we were going to have a language problem and I would have to allow for her misunderstanding me if I didn't talk slowly, present one idea at a time, or attempt to work with her in French.

Since my French was rusty, I thought I had better save it for later sessions, with short phrases so she could tell that I would work in her language when I could. At this point she trusted no one. We were starting from square one, with a language handicap to boot.

"I think that you must be very unhappy. Only unhappy people hurt themselves."

The tears fell now as she continued to look down at the rug.

"Yes . . . I am unhappy. But I don't know why. I have a good family. I have no reason for this. Maybe I'm crazy." She nodded to emphasize the finality of this appraisal.

"Maybe you need words instead of blades or knives."

She looked confused, not understanding the comparison that I was making. "How do words help the way you hurt?"

"Your words can build a bridge. Your bad feelings can travel over that bridge, away from you."

"To what place?"

"To me."

Simone was still puzzled. "How can my bad feelings leave me and go to you? Then you will have bad feelings."

"Your bad feelings don't have to hurt me. Maybe I will throw them away—something you can't do with them."

"But I don't know you. How can this happen?"

"It can happen as you get to know me for a longer and longer time. Talking together will build the bridge."

"You are a very strange man. I don't meet doctors that speak like you do."

"Strange–good, or strange–bad?"

With a large smile she answered, "Strange–very good."

"The next time you come here, maybe you will want to speak like that, too. Strange–very good."

"I would want to . . . if you don't change. I feel everyone is always changing to me. My feelings for everyone always change. Maybe if *you* don't change, my feelings about you won't change, and I will always want to come here. I hope so."

She came across as likable, sympathetic—and misunderstood. It seemed that this lack of understanding of her emotional pain made it harder for her needs to be met by her parents, and even by herself. My next step was to evaluate whether Simone had actually alienated them so effectively that they could neither reach her nor do anything "right" in her eyes.

At that point, I didn't know if Simone had really been disappointed by inconsistencies on the part of others or if she was suffering from a borderline personality disorder that would cause her continually to shift her feelings toward others from idealization to devaluation. Borderline personality disorder is a complex and serious illness, which produces extreme changeability of mood as well as reckless and impulsive behavior. I would, no doubt, find out, language barrier or no.

My first task would still be to develop the therapeutic relationship that I had called "a bridge" to get Simone to give up her cutting. Each symptom I could get her to give up would close off another outlet, and would eventually cause her to exchange acting out physically for talking about her feelings.

My first battle would be with her symptoms. In a sense, I had to get her to give them up for our relationship, because she did not at that point care enough about herself to give them up solely in her best interest.

This might be perceived as a controversial approach to therapy. Ideally, we all want to see patients give up their disorders for themselves. Most often, however, we are confronted with individuals who feel that they have no sense of self, or that they hate themselves. Our next task becomes winning their esteem, because we must use their esteem for us to help them value our appreciation of them. The third step in this process is to help them incorporate positive statements (which should be realistic) that we make about them into their own self-image. This is how the therapist can help patients feel better about themselves, produce pride in themselves, and raise their self-esteem.

Simone worked hard in therapy, her perfectionism spurring her to be my "best" patient. Often I would remind her that this was not a competitive process, just a place to learn about herself. She did not emerge as a borderline personality and gradually she was able to use my acceptance of her efforts and her feelings to counteract her negative self-image.

As the cutting subsided, the anorexia reemerged, which I had expected as it was her original diagnosis. Again, our work centered on dispelling Simone's ideas about the need for perfection, which had trapped her in two isolating behaviors, though fortunately not forever.

6

H O W   A N D   W H Y

T H E   D I S O R D E R   D E E P E N S

Most individuals do not develop psychological disorders to their fullest and most serious at the onset of their symptoms. In order to explain how the disorder deepens, it is helpful to compare self-mutilation with two other related disorders: obsessive-compulsive disorder and anorexia nervosa.

Obsessive-Compulsive Disorder: Michael

A twenty-year-old man called Michael explained to me during our initial interview that he became nearly housebound by having to repeat behaviors over and over again. These behaviors included hand-washing; drying his hands without "contaminating" them; tapping the center of surfaces (tables, countertops) five times before going on to the center of the next object; doing all of his "security-related" behaviors (checking different parts of his body) five times unless he thought that the behavior wasn't done just right, when he would have to check each one another five times; and clearing his throat five times before he spoke to anyone.

This all began after a bicycle accident he had at the age of fifteen. As a boy riding his bike, he became distracted by the spots of tar on the pavement. He noticed that when he rode his bike faster, the spots assumed the shape of long black lines. It amused him. One day he was nearly hypnotized by the lines and collided with a parked car so violently that he was thrown over the handlebars of his bike, lacerating his genitals as he flew forward. He landed on his hands and scraped both arms.

A middle-aged couple was in the car, in the process of pulling out of their parking space. They immediately got out, saw that there was no damage to their car, and walked over to Michael. The man lifted the boy up abruptly, pulling sharply under his arms. Michael then found himself face-to-face with the woman who had been in the passenger seat. She looked at his face with a startled expression, which led Michael to believe that his face might be badly injured, possibly even mutilated.

The man asked Michael if he was all right. He responded that he was, mostly in order to free himself of this overzealous good samaritan. As the couple drove away, Michael slowly walked over to a car window to examine his face, dreading what he might see. There was nothing wrong, no damage to his face. He checked further by looking in the rearview mirror of another parked car. Still nothing.

But Michael realized that he was experiencing severe pain from his groin and his fears intensified. What could he do? He couldn't examine his groin right there on the street. He was afraid to get back on his bike for fear that if he had damaged his genitals, the saddle seat of the bike would make things worse. He walked his bike home, wondering all the way back what damage had been done to him.

When he arrived home, he quickly went to his room to examine himself. All he could see were some small scratches, but he felt a soreness and a constant cramp or ache in the area. The next day, he noticed that his testicles were swollen and the ache had gotten worse. He was afraid that he would become sterile or physically impotent. Michael was not comfortable telling his parents about his worries since they were not the kind of family that discussed private matters, so he spent an anxious week checking himself several times a day. By the fourth day the swelling had gone down noticeably; at the end of the week it was almost completely gone, as was the discomfort he had been experiencing since the accident. Nevertheless, he continued to examine himself for months thereafter.

He began a series of superstitious behaviors before riding his bike which spread to the act of leaving the house before a ride. Soon he did these things even when he was not going to ride the bike. Michael's sense of danger had insinuated itself into more and more activities until it was always with him.

Perhaps if he had spoken to one of his parents, and had either been reassured or taken to a doctor immediately, he would not have developed these maladaptive behaviors in order to "protect" himself. By the time I saw him, he was entrenched in them—and severely impaired. The people closest to him had no leverage with which to compete with the feeling of security that his rituals gave him.

Anorexia Nervosa: Krista

Krista was thirteen years old when she first decided to lose weight. Her parents were both working at demanding jobs and they often came home from work worn out and late, just in time to eat dinner. Despite their long hours, they didn't or couldn't afford to hire help. Krista did all the shopping and cooking. There was very little personal talk between Kirsta and her exhausted parents. Krista spent her spare time reading the type of service magazines for girls that they mostly read between the ages of nine and thirteen.

(Readers of these magazines usually go on to women's fashion magazines after the age of thirteen.)

Krista was not getting any feedback about herself or even her cooking from her distracted and beleaguered parents, so she turned to these magazines in order to get some sort of appraisal of her adequacy. She quickly discovered that the most important achievement associated with adequacy was thinness.

To meet this standard, she began losing weight. At thirteen, she was five foot five and weighed one hundred and eight pounds, normal for her frame. After she had lost twenty pounds, unnoticed by her parents, a school nurse called home to inform them that their daughter weighed eighty-eight pounds and that this twenty-pound loss should be investigated.

The parents were mortified and embarrassed. They did not admit to the nurse or to their daughter that they hadn't even noticed her weight loss. They were both aware that as college-educated people, they should have identified this change in their daughter before it had gone this far. Following a medical examination which revealed no medical cause for her behavior, the pediatrician diagnosed Krista as having anorexia nervosa, and told her parents that she needed psychiatric care, which would hopefully prevent her from starving herself into medical danger.

By now Krista was so secure with her pattern of weight loss that it had become more important to her than the opinions of her parents or her doctor. It was unthinkable for her to choose to abandon her security system just because of their wishes, judgments, or even threats. She ultimately ended up in the eating disorder unit of a psychiatric hospital, where she regained the weight, only to lose and regain it repeatedly through two more hospitalizations.

It was clear to me that no one involved with Krista's treatment had formed a relationship or a connection with her that could compete with the comfort, satisfaction, and safety that her anorexia had provided. She was so mentally involved with regulating her eating, exercising, and elimination that avoiding gaining weight was almost all she thought about, even though she had been admonished that she would be in great danger if she didn't change her weight-losing patterns.

Krista was frequently asked rhetorically, "Don't you want to be pretty, and healthy?" She would not give up her dangerous behavior for herself; she didn't have enough self-esteem for that. She might give it up for someone else that she held in higher esteem. But she would be difficult to reach, since she had drifted so far away from even hoping for an important relationship that would make her feel safe and comforted.

In the case of both Michael and Krista, the length of time the patients used their maladaptive defenses for relief from psychological confusion, insecurity, or pain increased their dependence on their psychopathological behaviors. In each case, the person took a bit of truth and distorted it until their behavior was out of their own control. At the same time they were becoming entrenched in these behaviors, they were also increasing the distance between themselves and their families and peer groups. They became more and more emotionally disconnected from the people around them, which, like the chronic use of their symptoms, deepened the illness. Each became sicker, harder to reach, and more difficult to treat the longer his/her pain went unnoticed.

Self-Mutilation

What is the beginning of the loss of perspective that leads to cutting or burning oneself? Do we perceive a person who begins with nail-biting and then goes on to doing mild damage to her nailbeds by picking at them as being sick? Do we see the nervous habit of biting one's lip go out of control and lead to self-mutilation? Rarely, if ever.

In the examples involving both obsessive-compulsive disorder and anorexia nervosa, we saw a gradual transition from mental health to mental illness, followed by a deepening of that illness. Self-mutilation, on the other hand, often starts in its pathological or "sick" form immediately, within an already existing illness. It begins as a sick feature from its onset, but may develop or deepen into such a frequent and severe form that it overshadows the illnesses from which it sprang. When I state that self-mutilation starts as "sick," I mean that the illness does not evolve from a mild, acceptable form of behavior like nail-biting into picking up a blade, scissors, or match to harm oneself.

Reconciling Brain and Mind

Today, the chemical nature of the human brain is being understood as never before; yet it is the human mind that we inhabit and experience. We all try out new behaviors haltingly, awkwardly, full of concentration and hypervigilant. As we practice these behaviors repeatedly, we become less halting, less awkward, our need to concentrate is less necessary, and we grow more casual and more efficient at the same time. Whether it is learning to walk, swim, ride a bike, drive a car, or parent a child, the progression of the learning experience usually follows the same pattern.

When these are positive achievements, we call them **learning**. If they are destructive or self-destructive, we call them **disorders**. Though these behaviors are labeled disorders, they are born from the same mechanisms as positive learning. The major difference between the two is that positive, healthy learning is most often taught by one person to another person, instructively.

Maladaptive learning, on the contrary, is inferred and may be need-based, or copied from a role model without direct encouragement or instruction. This kind of learning is, in effect, self-taught. It is often unconscious as well. When one person is taught by another person, that child, adolescent, or adult remembers the teaching experience as well as the guidelines and limitations involved in attempting the new behavior. We usually can easily re-member who taught us how to swim, or cook. But the child who is learning by inference and not by instruction is often doing so in order to survive physical or emotional unpleasantness, and does not have the guidelines that will tell her what is enough, when she can stop, or when she will be safe. Take, for example, a ten-year-old girl told to stifle a sad feeling or fear, who then carries a box of fudge to her room and eats the whole thing. She has just taught herself comfort through binging.

As different as they appear to you and me, both of these kinds of learning are treated in the same way by the mind. That is, as the thoughtfulness involved in producing the skill or behavior is ab-breviated, the process becomes automatic. When the behavior, or skill, has been developed over a long period of time, we say that the person who does the positive behavior or performs the skill is "experienced." The experienced person will often seek to increase his or her skill by trying out more difficult forms of it—whether ice-skating, skiing, mountain climbing, or playing a musical in-strument.

Similarly, when a person who has developed a disorder that originated with negative, inferred learning has had this disorder for months or years, that person is more likely to push the self-destructive behavior further. For the self-mutilator, that means doing more damage to herself. This increased damage becomes in-corporated as normal or usual as it occurs slowly over a period of time.

Just as there are reasons attached to increasing achievements, to pushing skills to their limits, so the mind looks for further avenues to intensify disordered behavior. In the case of anorexia, it is:

—How thin can I get?
—How much weight can I lose?
—How much willpower do I have to deal with deprivation?

—How much attention can I attract?

—How much exercise can I do on very little nutrition?

In the case of self-mutilation, a slightly different set of rationales is applied to deepen the disordered behavior:

—How much pain can I take?

—How much disfigurement of my skin can I tolerate?

—How much bleeding can I stand?

In these cases, the individual has already established the disordered behavior, and now wants more relief, more satisfaction from it. The victim starts thinking like one who is addicted to a substance: more is better. The more disordered the behavior, the greater the escape from emotional pain.

The mind in each case has adjusted to the existing level of behavior or achievement, and is now seeking to increase intensity in order to maintain the rush of reaching the current level that was once new. Let us contrast two examples—one of early detection and one that was chronic.

Katerina and Carla

Katerina had started with small cuts on the underside of her arm. They were half an inch long and just deep enough to draw blood. Over a five-year period, she upped the ante to larger, deeper, and wider cuts. Sometimes she would resort to burns with a cigarette, match, or candle. Once she pressed a hot teapot full of boiling water against her thigh; another time she bit a gash in her own arm. By this point she was emotionally and mentally disintegrating into dissociated states and experiencing amnesia during the incidents. Her behavior went undiscovered for four long years.

Carla, fourteen, came into treatment for anorexia and depression. Her diagnosis had been made within the last year. I asked her if she cut herself.

"Sure, on my arms and breasts."

"How long have you been doing this?"

"For about three months."

"Why these two areas?"

"The skin is very sensitive and tender in both areas. You can get a lot of pain with very little damage."

"Why do you want the pain?"

"I'm the only one I allow myself to hurt."

"Does anyone else know?"

"That would defeat the whole purpose. It would hurt both my parents to find out I do this."

During the rest of Carla's first year of treatment, there were only two more incidents of cutting and they were much milder. In fact, the second incident was scratching, and the results were barely detectable. After that, they stopped entirely.

Early detection, as with nearly all developing problems (medical or psychiatric), offers the best prognosis and outcome, with the help of skilled treatment and a supportive environment. While Carla and I were working to reverse the development of self-mutilation, we were able to reduce the addictive behaviors that precede the formation of the disorder. From there we worked to fill the deficits in her emotional development that invited these symptoms.

With Katerina, it was a long time before we could get her to stay aware of her environment throughout a session, to focus on our dialogue, and even longer before we began to reduce and eventually stop her severe self-mutilations. It was two years before we got to the point I had reached with Carla in the first four months of treatment.

———————

The athlete who becomes a champion in her sport, or the businesswoman who becomes the most successful in her field, often become so invested in their field of expertise that they cannot focus on any other aspects of life, even their families.

A parallel situation develops with someone who is chronically or deeply involved in his or her disorder. That person becomes more difficult to reach and to develop a therapeutic relationship with. The double jeopardy here is that when the disorder is at its most dangerous, the patient is at her most inaccessible. The therapy must be skilled, strong, and as frequent as possible: twice a week outpatient.

The learning model outlined above helps us to avoid the pitfalls of suspecting the patient of being stubborn and uncooperative; of seeing the patient as so different, so sick, that she cannot be helped; or of becoming overwhelmed by her tenacious behavior. Later, I will explain and illustrate the treatment methods I have found to be effective in reversing this process. If the family and the therapist can both keep in mind that the terms **change** or **cure** refer to **rebuilding** and **reparenting**, then the damage can be stopped and reversed. The patient can be reparented so that her unhealthy defenses become unnecessary; the newly obsolete defenses can then be extinguished, and personality deficits filled in with the help of strong interpersonal connections.

7

ATTACHMENT PATTERNS

Attachment is a vital part of all human relationships, commonly defined as joining or binding by personal ties. Self-mutilators suffer from severe deficits in the ability to form personal attachments—to join others—whether it's to have fun, to talk seriously about each other, to talk personally about themselves, or to accept comfort and reassurance from another person.

The Benefits of Attachments

In order to truly understand the void that is left by a lack of personal attachments, perhaps we ought to look at the benefits derived from having the ability to form them. When a person can form attachments to others, it means that he or she is someone who is able to trust and to develop healthy dependencies. These kinds of connections between individuals allow us to be restored or supported when we are emotionally played out. Conversely, if a person has no attachments to others, he or she risks emotional depletion, pathological levels of obsessiveness, and the disorders associated with these conditions: phobias, depression, eating disorders, obsessive-compulsive disorder, and self-mutilation.

Of course, attachments, like many of the concepts we have addressed thus far, can be qualified as either "healthy" or "unhealthy." When someone has an unhealthy attachment, it is termed **fanatic** or **blind**.

People who are capable of forming healthy attachments have learned from their families that trustworthy, reliable attachments are possible. They know that positive experiences with others are achievable, and this kind of optimism dates back to their own childhood. Outside the psychological definitions, however, there exist a wide range of personal definitions for what constitutes a healthy attachment. Most of us find a workable medium—an attachment that incorporates both trust and distance to varying degrees.

The self-mutilator, on the other hand, is someone who has not found a workable medium, and usually does not have *any* healthy attachments to others. At the first therapy session with new patients, I generally ask them: "Whom do you trust? Whom can you lean on? Whom can you cry to about yourself?"

The most typical answer I get in response to this series of questions is, "Myself," followed by, "It's foolish and weak to depend on others because they'll probably let you down," or, "I'm safest trusting and depending on no one."

This type of response indicates that some event, circumstance, personality, or even a combination of all three, has thwarted the development of the restorative mechanisms of trust and dependency. If one cannot form trusting attachments, psychological or behavioral disorders, or both, follow. These disorders fill the void left by the lack of interpersonal relationships and serve as replacements for healthy attachments. This is nearly always the case in the personality development of the self-mutilator.

Kessa: Lonely at the Top

Kessa was a sophomore at an urban college. Her circumstances allowed her to exhaust herself both at academic tasks and in her involvement in successful, even glamorous businesses in the city. The combined productivity of her school and nonschool activities produced envy on the part of her friends. This envy came out as teasing about her "Superwoman" activity. Yet it seemed that almost no one Kessa's own age respected her, or appreciated her for her productivity and energy. Her parents continually expressed concern and disapproval that she wouldn't have a social life if she didn't ease up on her heavy load of schoolwork, extracurricular work, and internships. She did fall asleep in class, on the city buses, or any other time she sat still. While her parents fretted, her professors and the adults who supervised her outside school were charmed by her.

Kessa saw herself as a commodity that had to be continually honed in order to maintain success, otherwise, the rest of the world would somehow lose interest in her. At least she believed that. When she expressed the slightest signs of fatigue to her friends, rather than offer her support, they teased her and chided, "It's amazing you haven't dropped dead by now!" Her parents would admonish her for the fix she had gotten herself into, and wanted her to give up some of her commitments. It seemed that no one could simply be supportive. She turned to eating to compensate herself for the lack of support and nurturing from which she suffered. When her weight got too high for her to "look successful," according to her own interpretation of society's standards, Kessa began to purge.

She was referred to me for help with her bulimia when her roommates called her parents to tell them that they saw signs of this behavior. She began to cut herself when she felt upset, but was afraid that her roommates would catch her vomiting in the dorm bathroom. She gradually shifted her symptomatic behavior from binging and purging to cutting because it offered her more privacy.

Kessa entered the office dressed fashionably and exuding boredom from every facial muscle.

Since I had the feeling she had not come to the session on her own accord, I asked her, "Do you know why you were sent to see me?"

"For no valid reason," she assured me.

I decided to confront her seeming disinterest with the information I'd been given. "I don't care how hard you work, or how many activities you participate in. That sounds like good, productive, energetic stuff. I'm thinking that you don't know how to balance your work with leisure, or restore your energy output. Your mother made it clear that you have at least one symptom of being overwhelmed and overworked."

"What did you mean by 'at least' one when you were talking about me having a symptom?"

"Well, it's clear to your friends and your parents that you are engaging in purging, a nice name for vomiting, after you eat. You are probably doing this to prevent weight gain because you are eating more than you can without gaining weight."

Suddenly, anger flashed across her face. The boredom was gone. "Wait a minute! I just got here and you're already saying that I eat like a pig!"

"No. I'm suggesting that the information I was given, if it's correct, means that you're eating beyond hunger and that means something is wrong. We call that 'symptomatic eating'; it makes up for something that you need from other people but aren't getting. I also noticed you took exception to my remark about you having 'at least' one identified symptom. That causes me to wonder what other self-harming behavior you're engaged in."

"I'm not engaged, as you put it, in any self-harming behavior." Her eyes welled up though she wasn't actually crying.

"Do you cut yourself?"

She jumped nearly out of her chair. "What do you mean, do I cut myself?"

I leaned back and spoke softly and casually, as if I were talking about something harmless, commonplace, and ordinary. "Well, let's say you're full of tension and fatigue. Two girls are showering in the dorm bathroom. It's just before dinner and some of the girls are going on dates. There's not much privacy anywhere. Everyone's doing their nails in the lounge or the living room to your suite. Suddenly you discover that you're alone in your bedroom. You grab a knife, a fork, or a scissors, and in the blink of an eye, you make a cut on the underside of your forearm and quickly put down whatever you used. Even if someone walked in right afterward you could always shout, 'Damn!', blame the cut on the corner of the dresser, and walk out of the room to dress the wound . . . Hmmm?" I nodded my head.

She stared at me, dumbstruck by what I had just said, and just as surprised by how casually I said it.

She started to stare blankly out the window behind me. Then she looked at me. "Pretty good," she said. "And what if it's true?"

"Do you want to show me your arms?"

Kessa paused as if she were contemplating an infinite number of retorts. Her expression turned from puzzled to mind-racing to weary—maybe weary of keeping so many things a secret.

"So what if I have done that—I'm not saying that I have—but just what if?"

"I would say that means you're burned out but don't know what to do about it or who to turn to."

"Who to turn to? There's never anyone to turn to! My fellow students think that my hard work is a joke; my parents think that I'm being stupid, showing poor judgment. If I can get my mother serious about me for more than a second, and God forbid I cry, she starts crying along with me. That's a big help. And if my dad was ever home from work for five minutes without 'making business calls,' he wouldn't *listen,* he'd just try to come up with a perfectly logical and totally irrelevant 'solution' for everything. There *is* no one to turn to!"

"I guess that's why you're here."

"What do you mean?" She was still angry, but tearful now too.

"Well, if no one knows what you need, no one who you know yet, we'll have to find out and address that here."

"How the hell—excuse me—can you just sit there and say that as if I'm a customer at the dry cleaner's and you want to know if I want some starch or not?"

"Maybe because it's my life's work. Maybe because helping people is my life's work," I said in a tone of mock casualness.

She looked puzzled again and shook her head. "Well, I don't know how you can figure out what to do with someone like me."

"You don't seem foreign or unfamiliar to me."

She giggled. "Well, you must lead some horrible life."

"You don't have much self-esteem, do you?"

"Through the floor. You'll find it in the basement."

I decided to respond playfully as a break from the intense discussion. "I guess we'll have to find it, stand it up, and starch it, like at the dry cleaner's."

She smiled and nodded. "That's pretty cool. You really think that's possible, that you can do it?"

"I wouldn't even suggest it if I didn't have a large box of starch in the closet."

"I'm not so easy to get along with, you know."

"Thanks for the warning."

Kessa was without secure attachments, yet by the end of our first session she betrayed her hope that it would be possible to develop at least one: with her therapist. It would be difficult to create a prognosis scale to measure hopefulness to hopelessness about establishing trust, attachment, and dependency. If we could, Kessa would fall on the hopeful side, which gave her a good prognosis.

But before she left the office, I had a request to make. "Can I see those arms now?"

Her shoulders dropped. "Okay."

She awkwardly unbuttoned the cuffs of her sleeves. Her right arm was clean, but the left forearm was cluttered with cuts and scratches (some looked as though they had been made with fingernails when there probably was no time to obtain a cutting instrument). She looked at her arm, then at me. "Pretty ugly, huh?"

"No, just sad for you, that this is the only way you know how to say, 'Ouch, I hurt, I need.' "

"Well, can I make another appointment, or am I too horrible to help?"

"Of course you can come back—for years if you want to."

Self-Esteem and Attachment

While Kessa and I did discuss the topic of being helped, we did not explicitly discuss the concepts of trust and dependency, or even attachment. We would first have to form a connection that would give these concepts real meaning before we discussed them. At our initial session, a discussion about these issues would have been purely intellectual. Intellectual discussion does not serve to create the kind of relationship that fosters the development of trust, dependency, and attachment.

The **therapeutic relationship** is of utmost importance here. If the therapist can prove to the patient that he is both worthy of her trust and dependable enough to form an attachment, then the patient can take what she has learned outside the office, and build positive attachments with others as well.

What transpired between Kessa and myself during our first session was implicit. My talk and tone suggested that she could risk attachment and trust. Her talk suggested her cynicism, but also a fear that these ideas could leave her vulnerable to harm. It is ironic to think that Kessa, who was harming herself the most, could be frightened about someone being capable of harming her. Of course, she preferred the harm she knew to the harm she didn't.

I continue to find that a self-mutilator has a poor ability to form attachments to others while, paradoxically, she has an excellent ability to encourage others to form attachments to her. She can be an excellent listener, and nurturer, to others.

Kessa had many friends, but the relationships were all one-sided. She knew them on a deep, personal level, while they never even asked about her. This arrangement suited her perfectly.

Self-mutilators rarely allow others to achieve emotional closeness to them. They have a powerful sense that they could only be harmed by the closeness of others. Some of them have experienced harm at the hands of those they were supposed to trust the most—their parents.

In cases where actual physical or sexual abuse has occurred, the self-mutilator's original adaptive behavior of emotional distancing makes sense. Though this defense will become obsolete as she outgrows the age and circumstance where there was a real threat, she will continue to keep her guard up as a result of what she learned in her formative years.

Sometimes the abuse is purely verbal. The child is insulted and criticized more often than she is complimented and supported. In this scenario, the same negative set of expectations of other people is created. With verbal abuse, the damage to one's willingness and ability to form attachments is slightly less severe and leads to fewer and milder self-destructive symptoms. **Low self-esteem**, however, will be a lingering result of abuse whether it is verbal or physical.

Low Self-Esteem

Low self-esteem has a direct impact on patterns of personal attachment. The individual with low self-esteem is prone to forming attachments with persons who are abusive to her or needier than she is. She believes that she deserves this behavior and unconsciously or unwittingly invites it. Another feature of the self-mutilator's personality, then, may be the tendency to establish abusive relationships that are reminiscent of "home," familiar, and in keeping with her childhood experiences. One component of this phenomenon is that security and pain have become fused.

This fusion of pain with security causes her to "treat" her feelings of insecurity, loneliness, and fear of abandonment with self-inflicted pain, which temporarily produces security and even tranquility. The self-mutilator, then, is someone who trusts only her pain because she connects it with "home." When she is older and in emotional trouble, she does not turn to another person to express her grief, but to the pain, because she can assure its presence. It is the most reliable relationship in her life, and the most familiar.

How Shame Interferes with Attachment

We have seen, in previous chapters, individuals who have committed acts against themselves which caused them pain and did physical damage to their bodies. In the cases of Jessica (chapter 2), who was sexually abused, and Tracy (chapter 5), who was beaten with her father's belt, we saw how such individuals have explicitly used this physical pain and self-destruction to make their psychological pain go away.

Any attempts that these young women made at self-disclosure were accompanied by shame. Both had difficulty describing their behavior, and in both cases they had never shared this information with anyone else. Each of them took approximately a year in therapy (following years with other therapists) to finally let out these secret behaviors they had been so ashamed of.

In Jessica's case, her behavior involved irritating her genitals with soap. This is not something that most people could readily discuss with a friend. Tracy's behavior of cutting herself with the buckle of the same belt her father had used to beat her with was equally difficult for her to reveal. Imagine the shame at having to discuss this information, and the fear of the listener's possible re-action to it. This gives us some idea of how a self-mutilator's iso-lation and lack of personal attachments become a self-perpetuating cycle.

Another factor that comes into play is the effect that the years of secrecy—the years of hiding self-mutilating behavior—has on the developing personality. The sense of shame spreads from the specific act of cutting to a general sense of shame about oneself. For Jessica, this constant state of being ashamed, coupled with the shame surrounding the original acts of childhood rape that she en-dured, combined to create a general sense of self-loathing. The conflict caused her continually to sabotage any chance of success she might have at any job, or in any personal relationship. This am-bivalence came out in her therapy when she became sulky and an-swered questions by equivocating, thus stalling the progress of the therapy. Unconsciously, she may have felt that she did not deserve success, even in overcoming her psychological problems.

This kind of patient poses special difficulties since she is both a danger to herself and a saboteur to those who wish to help her. She is constantly fighting the attachment she wishes for with her therapist. She knows, intellectually, that he is not a danger, but psychologically and emotionally he *does* represent a danger because trusting him would cause her to reorganize and possibly give up her defenses. This last danger can be the most threatening of all.

In some cases, the fear is not that an attachment to the thera-pist would lead to an undeserved cure, or the dismantling of her coveted symptoms, but that the therapist would be rejecting. As we saw with both Tracy and Jessica, one reason the self-mutilator lacks personal attachments is that she avoids even attempting them for fear that if someone got to know her, they might be shocked, repulsed, and rejecting of her.

This fear extends to the psychotherapist as well as friends. Recently, I have received several calls from parents of girls who have been cutting themselves. In each case, they have consulted non-medical psychotherapists (only psychiatrists have a medical degree). When the therapist was told that the patient was a cutter, they declined the case, expressing that they didn't "have any experience with this kind of problem," or that the child should be seen by a psychiatrist. This made both parent and child feel rejected, lost, and hopeless about obtaining successful treatment.

Like the glib Mildred (chapter 4), who insisted that she was "too much" for me because she felt she had been too much for everyone else (or so they allowed her to believe), including three previous therapists, the rejected patient feels that she cannot be helped, that she is a psychiatric "freak." This sort of discouragement can worsen her symptoms. It also throws into turmoil the secret wish for a helpful attachment. Ultimately, what I call the **attachment-dependency-trust axis** is crucial to recovery from cutting or burning behaviors and all the personality deficits and disorders behind them. The task of the therapist—and ideally of the parents, too—is to form a relationship based on trust that encourages dependency and leads to a healthy attachment.

This is the only way the patient will finally find the courage to abandon her self-harming behaviors and learn to form such a healthy attachment.

8

THE BENEFITS OF
SELF-WOUNDING

Pain as the Goal

It takes quite a stretch of the imagination to understand why a person might seek out pain and her own wounding as a solution to her mental and emotional suffering. Though we all put up with the pain inherent in dentistry, say, or childbirth, or surgery, pain is the unwanted by-product of these experiences. The pain is endured for a positive outcome—the repairing of a tooth, the birth of a baby. The role of dentistry and obstetrics is to minimize the pain; in self-mutilation, pain is the *goal,* not the by-product.

A certain amount of pain in life is inevitable. If we try to insulate ourselves from all pain, we become numb. **Repression**, which is the process of pushing unacceptable feelings out of one's awareness, doesn't really make negative feelings go away, but rather will channel them into disguises. Sometimes these disguises show up as psychosomatic symptoms like headaches, backaches, stomachaches, high blood pressure, and so on. Other times the disguises are psychological symptoms that may take the form of moodiness, depression, or anxiety. These may, in turn, develop into serious behavior disorders like anorexia, trichotillomania (hair-pulling), or self-mutilation.

Cutting: An Act of Anger

A cutter who has been abused often employs the psychological defense of self-mutilation. She is in fact using physical pain, with which she is familiar, to ward off emotional pain. One of my patients—Lynn—as a child experienced frequent and extreme sexual abuse. She was in a constant state of emotional pain. This kind of pain is overwhelmingly complex and vague, and because it is undefined, it cannot be reasoned with, it has no name. Lynn's emotional pain seems to have an infinite life. In order to control it, she creates physical pain, which is finite and results in a state of calm.

The infliction of pain on oneself is often a substitute for anger toward another, and possibly the unconscious desire to inflict pain on that other person. Consciously inflicting pain on another person is forbidden for a variety of reasons: the fear of the destruction of a needed person, or the fear of loss of love or care by that person. So, cutting may indeed be an angry act, which temporarily (and fictitiously) redresses the cutter's grievance with the other person.

Cutting: An Act of Self-Medication

When the body is injured, hormones called **endorphins** are released to fight anxiety, agitation, and depression.* The self-mutilator may be combining depression, anxiety, and past history (during which she was the recipient of harm at the hands of others) in order to become the architect of her own pain. By deter-

---

*See Hans Heubner, *Endorphins and Anorexia* (New York: W. W. Norton, 1994).

mining which punishments to dole out, she can take charge of her worst experiences. The chemical interplay can produce an addiction to the "drugs" manufactured by one's own body. This suggests an attempt at **self-medication** of one's mood disorders.

When we see a patient who cuts, burns, or in some other way does physical damage to herself—exempting direct suicide attempts, with which self-mutilation has sometimes been confused—she is acting in a state of severe mental illness.

What Is the Cutter Thinking?

We have already seen some of the different ways that individuals injure themselves. As great as the variety of tools and methods used by these self-injurers, equally varied are their states of mind when they either set out to hurt themselves, or do so impulsively without premeditation.

There are those, like Lynn, who are a living example of someone whose earliest interpersonal experiences are interlaced with pain. They slip into the trancelike states I have mentioned, and some don't even remember the event, although most do. Here is Lynn's description of one such episode:

"I don't remember what happened. I just know that I 'woke up' parked on the side of the road and it was four o'clock. I was sure it was one o'clock, but I had lost three hours. My left arm was high on the steering wheel and it was covered with nearly dried blood, running from near my wrist all the way down to my underarm. Some had overrun my short-sleeve shirt and gone down the side of it. It seemed like a lot of blood, but after years of doing this, I looked to see if it had formed a pool anywhere. It hadn't, so I knew that I hadn't lost a dangerous amount, but it looked so gross!

"I found my little penknife on the seat beside me: the blade and handle were covered with blood. It was all so sloppy. That may sound crazy to you, but it matters to me how I do it. It's kind of like being double out of control. Cutting myself may sound crazy or out of control to you, but *how* I do it should be *in* control. If I 'space out' on my bed and wake up three hours later, it's like I took a nap—not so bad. But if I 'wake up' behind the wheel on the side of the road, maybe I picked up a hitchhiker who raped me and left. Then I have to wonder, did I space out in the middle of the rape, if one happened, and if I did, did he quit and leave or not?

"So then I have to check my clothes and underwear for signs of 'him', whether I'm disheveled or not, whether there's semen there or not. I have to treat this like a police investigation—but I never would go to the police. I have found evidence of rape before; not this time. If I went to the police, I would have nothing to tell them except, 'Pardon me, but I'm given to amnesia and I was raped during my last episode. Can you help me?' How stupid and crazy would that sound?"

Trading Pains

Lynn's self-mutilation would continue to benefit her by acting as a constant shield to separate her emotionally from the assaults she remembered experiencing during childhood, as well as the feeling that there was "nobody out there" who would ever protect her. Since talking about this in therapy might produce those old feelings, I was concerned that the therapy itself not provoke additional cutting. We kept "memory discussions" down to ten minutes of any session and monitored her behavior between sessions.

Lynn had been raped by her baby-sitter's boyfriend from the time she was six until she was eight. Like so many other child victims, she was told by the seventeen-year-old boy that he would kill her if she informed her mother. Lynn's mother had to work full time to support them since her father left them penniless when Lynn was five and a half. She was not only afraid of the boy's threat but understood that if her mother had no baby-sitter, she could not go to work, and then they would be out on the street, as her mother had often said when Lynn asked, even pleaded with her mother not to leave for work on a given day.

Since there was no one to protect her, Lynn had to retreat inside herself and find ways to cope with the nightmare her life had become since her father left. She did what many incest victims do who feel hopelessly trapped: They "go away" during the assault. If she is lucky, she invokes amnesia so well that she doesn't remember the event. Then, if the assaults continue repeatedly, she begins to utilize amnesia for other and lesser conflicts. Eventually, it becomes involuntary a good part of the time.

In these situations, Lynn's cutting herself without feeling it became the first step in her "going away" by proving to herself that the "mental Novocaine," the numbness, had taken effect. The cutting would take place after an assault. The rape of a child by an adult is not only terrifying but extremely painful. It is this pain caused by the rape that is used as the trigger to invoke "going away," "spacing out," or creating a dissociative state—**amnesia**—to spare the victim her terror, pain, humiliation, and feelings of helplessness. These feelings would create deeper flights from reality, perhaps even permanent flights, or **psychosis**.

Other cutters are not necessarily fleeing the grotesque experiences suffered by Lynn or Jessica (chapter 2). Theirs may be milder physical abuse by parents.

I am aware that the word "milder" when discussing parental- or sibling-generated abuse appears to degrade the intensity and horror of this kind of experience, but I am trying to create a continuum necessary to distinguish between levels of symptoms, of mental illness, and the environmental provocations involved.

As problems continue for the cutter, she retreats further into herself. In this way, she can block out past memories and experiences without turning to another person for help. Her childhood experiences have taught her that others are never much help or protection. As she turns more deeply and more frequently inward, she simultaneously cuts more often and more severely. At the severer end of this process, Lynn would be prone to go into dissociative states to protect herself from her feelings more often. At this point we would diagnose hers as a **dissociative disorder** as well. This places her at the most pathological end of the continuum.

The American Psychiatric Association defines dissociative disorder as follows:

> The essential feature is sudden temporary alteration in the normally integrative functions of consciousness, identity, or motor behavior. If the alteration occurs in consciousness, important personal events cannot be recalled. If it occurs in identity, either the individual's customary identity is temporarily forgotten and a new identity is assumed, or the customary feeling of one's own reality is lost and replaced by a feeling of unreality.★

In the case of **nondissociative cutting**, where numbness is not the goal but feeling the pain is, I often find the provocations to be related to feelings about others in the person's life. Perhaps the nondissociative cutter is marginally healthier than the **dissociative cutter**.

Love Hurts

Sonia (chapter 3), the cellist whose mother dug her fingernails into Sonia's bow arm when she made mistakes, still loved and was attached to her mother. She also feared and distrusted her mother. When her mother said that the punishment was "for your own good," Sonia tried to believe her. She incorporated this idea so that when she made mistakes but was not in her mother's presence, she would either dig her own nails into her bow arm, bite herself

---

★I have used the older description found in the *Diagnostic and Statistical Manual*'s 3rd edition (1980), since I believe it to be more concise for our purposes.

there (she did this once in my office waiting room after a session where she felt she did a poor job answering my questions), or scratch or cut herself with a penknife small enough to fit on her key chain but effective enough to draw lots of blood.

Sonia was psychiatrically on the cusp, exhibiting signs relating to both the dissociating and the nondissociating self-mutilator. She spaced out, but at the same time needed the pain as part of her "conscience," or connection to her mother. Her behavior was intended both to maintain this connection and to express her self-loathing, using her mother's criteria. She was not conscious of or able to feel anger toward her mother's Draconian rules for failure. This would come later in her therapy.

Sonia was also bulimic. When she purged, she was unconsciously expressing anger not at herself but at her parents. When she became conscious of her anger toward them, she gave up her bulimia. (This is not to state that anger toward parents is the only reason for the development of bulimia.)

The Payoff of Pain

Carla (chapter 6), who suffered from anorexia and depression, cut her arms and breasts when she was angry at herself, or felt anger toward her parents but believed them both to be too emotionally frail to deal with her hostility. Their marital discord made each of them unhappy: her father developed a stutter and her mother became withdrawn. Carla's cutting was designed to create the most pain with the least damage to herself.

This satisfied Carla's need for an outlet for her disappointment and anger without directly hurting her parents. She stated earlier that the areas that she was cutting were selected because the skin was most sensitive to pain. Carla's cutting falls into the nondissociative, non-amnesia-inducing, consciously pain-seeking category. This part of the spectrum suggests a sad, angry, but more mentally integrated personality than the earlier examples.

The Exhibitionist—and Secondary Gain

At the opposite end from the dissociative cutter is the cutter who is not at all secretive about her activities, and sometimes even exhibitionistic. She is damaging herself in full view of the world. When others around her find out what she is doing to herself, they become frightened for her, sometimes angry at her, while expressing their worry and helplessness to her. This intense focus and attention is gratifying in its own way, despite the fact that anger, worry, and fear are what we call **negative attention**. She also feels more powerful when she commands this type of attention. This emotional dynamic is known as **secondary gain**, a familiar concept in child psychology.

Think, for example, of the child who misbehaves in school because he's not getting enough attention; singling him out for frequent scoldings makes him feel important. The ability to stop the teacher and the class from normal functioning and focus on him rewards him with feelings of power. The gain is called "secondary" because the primary reason for misbehaving is usually another problem, such as a learning disability or a troubled home. Secondary gain occurs when the child starts to notice the benefits that occur as a result of misbehavior. Thus the scoldings reinforce, rather than discourage the bad behavior, by making him feel important and powerful.

When the cutter experiences secondary gain, she is getting benefits because of her sick behavior. Secondary gain is **unconscious**, which means that she has *no awareness of her motives*. The cutter who exhibits rather than hides her symptoms is not a phony. She has simply discovered that negative attention is better than none. Also she has attained a sense of powerfulness which may be in sharp contrast to the helpless feelings of her childhood.

If we have to decide who is the more pathological, or sicker, the dissociative self-mutilator or the secondary gain self-mutilator, the former is in even more trouble in terms of recovery. But we must understand that all self-mutilators are in serious psychological trouble.

Becoming Comfortable with Pain

If, as a reader, you have been able to stay with this text until now, without skipping pages that are too painful for you, then your capacity to deal with the graphic details of self-mutilating behavior has been expanded. In fact, you have probably been desensitized to cutting, burning, and bleeding far beyond where you were when you started this book.

It is much the same for the cutter. She gradually becomes desensitized to her existing repertoire of self-harming behavior. Unfortunately, she has increased her capacity to become dependent on greater self-harm, while you as a reader have become capable of coping more easily with this subject. It is vital for the therapist who treats such a patient to understand this phenomenon, because reactions of shock or dismay about the cutting make her feel incomprehensible to the very person she has turned to for understanding and help.

As the connection between patient and therapist becomes stronger, the benefits of self-wounding become weaker. Later, we will see how the therapist can finally help the patient to exchange her pain for personal attachment.

9

THE VALUE OF PAIN
IN OUR CULTURE

If one is in training for a competition, whether a piano competition or the Olympics, it is considered reasonable to develop a regime of activity that takes up an exorbitant amount of one's time. This time is perceived as reasonable because it is devoted to a social goal toward which others will be devoting similar amounts of time. In addition, the activity is supervised by a coach, so that the seemingly excessive demand is monitored by another person.

When runners reach a certain point of exhaustion, dubbed "the Wall," they are advised to push beyond it until they get their second wind. This exemplifies the cultural approval of the concept behind competitive performance: How much pain or exhaustion can you take? So we see that it is our society, not the lone individual, that has set the standards for training as well as for victory.

If an individual takes it upon herself to see how much pain she can endure, inflicting that pain by intentionally wounding her body, we call this "illness." Specifically, we call it "self-mutilation."

There is no socially acceptable goal; there are no limitations; no one else is involved. If this self-inflicted pain were to occur on an island inhabited by a lone person, we might even designate it "entertainment" of a desperate sort, or compensation for the lack of interpersonal stimulation available. But if it happens amid others who *are* available for contact, or stimulation, then it is designated as being outside the area of good mental health.

In much the same manner, one who is starved by a famine, emaciated by that starvation, is not thought of as mentally ill but rather as a victim of environment and circumstance. It is when someone starves herself amid plenty, with no restrictions, that we define this as mental illness, specifically, anorexia nervosa.

The intense desire to prove to one's self "How much pain can I take?" with no outside motivation, or limits, suggests that the individual has lost all realistic sense of goals, or solutions to her problems.

The self-mutilator is usually a step further removed from cultural suggestion than the anorexic or obsessive-compulsive-disordered individual. The latter two often began with a culturally acceptable goal. For one, it was to do things diligently, meticulously; for the other, it was to lose some weight. Both began that way but then were unable to stop, even as their behavior reached pathological and self-destructive levels. The self-mutilator, on the other hand, does not usually begin with a specific cultural message as the basis of her behavior but invents this behavior spontaneously and impulsively, out of a need to seek relief from mental pain.

No Pain, No Gain

Shari was twelve years old when she came into treatment. She was a committed gymnast who had attended her first tryouts for the local gymnastics team at the age of nine. Her coach saw her as having a powerful though small body. He interviewed her parents, to see if Shari's hereditary musculature could be determined from their appearance. He requested that both parents be present at an afternoon interview scheduled in late August, before the term began, telling them that he wanted their approval for the "strenuous dedication" he would require of their daughter.

The warm August day provided the incentive for the light, casual clothing they would wear, revealing the muscular shoulders, arms, and legs the coach was hoping to see on Shari's parents. He was not let down. With his encouragement, both told stories of their high school and college athletic exploits, and of rooting enthusiastically for their older son on the high school football team. The coach was delighted. He had parental encouragement, parental role-modeling, and a bonus of hereditary musculature.

Shari learned fast and well. She was excellent on the bar, the horse, and at all manner of somersaults. But after the first two years, Shari's mother read an article on the danger to physical growth when girls engage in intensive gymnastics throughout puberty. Shari's mother was five foot seven, and her husband six foot three. Shari was not growing at a rate that suggested she would reach her mother's height. Her pediatrician indicated at her next school checkup that Shari was in the lowest eighth percentile of height for eleven-year-olds. Her mother was shocked.

"How could ninety-two percent of children be taller than my daughter when my husband and I are both relatively tall people?" she asked the doctor.

He responded with a query: "I've noticed that Shari's musculature is quite developed, even overdeveloped, for her age. Is she involved in athletics to a great degree?"

"She is involved in gymnastics, and I know this year the girls have started lifting weights to increase their prowess in different events. The coach even requested—or it might be more accurate to say demanded—that we get her a set of dumbbells for extra practice at home. We drew the line when she requested a barbell."

The pediatrician explained that nothing was wrong with their daughter medically. She was in good health, though surprisingly short, considering her parents' respective heights, but she might have a growth spurt that would make all this a moot point. He asked whether there was anything in Shari's behavior that worried her parents, such as friends, social play, anything at all? On her way home in the car, his question stayed in Shari's mother's mind—she *was* worried about Shari's situation.

Mrs. A. reported to her husband what the pediatrician had told her about her daughter's height and the discussion they had had about her involvement in gymnastics. They called Shari in and broached the subject of lessening her involvement in gymnastics, and Shari became what they later described as "hysterical." In a pre-interview consultation, Mr. and Mrs. A. told me that Shari even threw things randomly around the room, including her five-pound dumbbell, which punctured the wall at the two points where the disks hit.

Mr. and Mrs. A. consulted me at the suggestion of their pediatrician after he saw Shari the following year for a checkup and discovered that she had grown less than an inch. During the year in between checkups Shari's parents had been unable to persuade their daughter to decrease her involvement in gymnastics, and she had in fact increased it. They were feeling helpless but were afraid to remove her from the program. The coach had reassured them that Shari wasn't working harder than the other girls he trained but she was doing better. He told Shari that he was considering her for captain of the team after her twelfth birthday.

Feeling outnumbered by their daughter and her coach, and possibly other members of the team as well, the parents finally sought help. As Mrs. A. put it, "She has no other life outside of gymnastics. And with puberty on the way, I don't see how she will move on to anything like a normal adolescence."

Mr. A. spoke next. "Shari has been told that we never intended for her to spend her young life pursuing an Olympic Gold Medal and we see that it's narrowed her life and may have permanently stunted her growth. Shari replied that if her growth is permanently stunted, 'It's too late anyway!' She is quite emphatic. We have also discovered that she has scratchmarks on both her upper arms. We asked if she had gotten into an argument with another girl. She shrugged off the question, saying that it happened when she slid against a piece of equipment. We can both see that the parallel lines on each arm are in a configuration which could only come from scratching herself."

"What is your reaction to her scratching herself like that?" I asked him.

"We can't tell if something's gone wrong with her gymnastics, or she's trying to punish us to ward off our attempts to reduce her activity there, or if she's angry or getting emotionally disturbed from the whole situation," Mr. A. said anxiously.

"We know that this age is full of changes for most girls and it's hard for us to tell if this is the beginning of something terrible or just part of puberty. What worries us most is we know that she's lying to us about the scratches, and worse than that, she backs us down because she's so adamant about her lies. Then, *bang!* her bedroom door slams. We know her coach doesn't know about the scratches and that we might jeopardize her chances of becoming captain of the team if he thinks we're withdrawing her involvement. So we are scared of having a sick child, and guilty about getting her started in this whole business nearly three years ago. I must admit we're also afraid of Shari's anger and unhappiness if it turns out that we ruin what she has accomplished for nothing."

Mrs. A. took up the story. "We know how hard the coach pushes all the girls—you know, 'No pain, no gain,' and all that rubbish. I'm afraid that she's become so good at 'pain' that she's got all of it mixed up with 'gain,' and she may be using pain in a cock-eyed way to feel like she's achieving something."

Shari's mom had interpreted the situation correctly. Her daughter had become part of a subculture that aligns pain with achievement. Even though the nature of the pain specified in the well-known sports slogan is the result of the struggle to perfect an exercise, it's not a big leap to apply the use of pain in other ways; to resolve inner conflicts and problems, for instance.

Shari was coaxed into coming to see me by her mother. Shari, no doubt, believed that seeing me would get her parents off her back and finally stop them from interfering with her gymnastics.

She entered the office with a sturdy, erect posture, stating by her body language that there was nothing wrong with her, and her parents were just two anxious people who couldn't cope with her success at gymnastics. I gestured to the couch and chairs; she sat down on the straightback chair, the one I call "the resistance chair."

I was aware that the person who had influenced her most for the past three years—her coach—was direct and forceful. So I introduced myself briefly and then stated, "This appointment has been made because your parents believe that you have begun to hurt or damage yourself as a way of resolving your conflicts, that is, whatever bothers you." I asked her to roll up her sleeves.

Looking more anxious, she did so. Four parallel tracks appeared on each arm.

Rolling up my own left sleeve, I took my right hand, and, using my four fingers, made four scratches on my left arm in the same place as her deeper, red scratchmarks on her left arm. I didn't say anything but waited for her response.

She stared at me in disbelief. She went on staring at my arm with its pale scratches, then looked at her own arm with its red, angry scratches. Tears began to flow. She remained silent for a few moments, then looked up at me sadly. "Am I crazy?"

I told her, of course, that she wasn't crazy. That she was trying to solve what bothered her by pushing herself even harder, as she'd learned to do in the past three years. At the same time she was telling herself to accept the by-products of her efforts, fatigue and pain—especially pain.

"You have been taught that if you ache, that means you've tried hard enough. You have mistakenly interpreted that to mean that the 'ache' is the solution to problems. Even an achievement in it-self."

"Well, sometimes I feel so bad that I don't know what to do. At least I didn't do the kind of damage that would prevent me from my workout." She looked at her arm again. "See, they're only scratches. They hurt when I did them, but they won't stop me from being strong and coordinated on the mats."

"We should make what upsets you into words."

"What if the words sound stupid or bad?"

"They usually just sound stupid or bad in your head, before you've said them to someone else who understands them, then they don't sound that way and you feel better."

She looked at me, curiously and timidly. "Is that why people go to therapy?"

I nodded.

"Do you know what they are, these thoughts and feelings that get you so upset?"

"I think I know some of them. If I tell them to you, then I won't want to scratch myself anymore?"

"I think that the better you get at figuring out what they are, and then telling them to me, the less you'll be tempted to hurt yourself."

Shari was identified early in her disorder. She was also very young. These factors allow a patient to be more receptive to her therapist's suggestions and less resistant to treatment. It was clear to me that Shari used self-mutilation as a way of keeping her doubts and fears about herself in check. There had been no time for nor-mal adolescent emotions in her highly pressured life as the star of her team.

Shari's use of scratching to punish herself for faltering and to reinforce her gymnastic training served as a red flag to her parents that she was in trouble. At this point of early intervention, she has only a tentative investment in her behavior. If she can form a strong therapeutic alliance with me, I can gradually help her to communicate her feelings. This process would compete with her need to hurt herself.

In Part Two of this book, we will see how this actually plays out in treatment.

The Hero Disguise

Brian was a senior at a competitive college. He was captain of the wrestling team, a cross-country runner, and a weightlifter. Aches and pains were no strangers to Brian. After a cross-country run, sometimes his legs hurt so badly that he had to walk downstairs backwards. Arm and chest pains from benchpressing prompted the purchase of a backpack; he was too sore to carry his books from class to class. Painful knots in his neck and back muscles after a wrestling match would have him on an athletic massage table for an hour a day.

Brian always understood that unlike a basketball player, he could not make a living after college as a wrestler, runner, or weightlifter. Yet these activities took up so much of his time that his grade point average was suffering. He was sent to therapy by his wrestling coach, who was notified by the dean of students that Brian had been kicking in windowpanes on the ground floor of the administration building. He was caught when he cut the top of the arch of his foot so badly that he severed tendons and needed orthopedic surgery in order to regain the use of his toes again, to walk properly. The surgeon noticed that in addition to the crippling wound he was repairing, Brian had many other long scars across the tops of both arches. Apparently, this last cut was the first one he could not "walk away from."

Brian was referred to me by the student counseling center for what the doctor thought was delinquent behavior. It turned out to be quite a different matter.

I explained to Brian at our first meeting that the surgeon had found many cuts on his foot, and that his socks seemed to have a reddish tinge that looked like it couldn't be washed out. I asked if he would please take off his sneakers so I could see his socks.

Brian was surprised by my request but nevertheless took off his sneakers to reveal white athletic socks with a pinkish hue. "This pair too, huh?" I commented.

"What do you mean?" He looked hurt.

"The report that accompanied the doctor's report was from the dean. It stated clearly that you were thought to be kicking in windows on the ground floor of the administration building. I don't think you've got a beef with the administration since they have given you a full scholarship, haven't they?"

"Yes, but what do you mean by kicking in windows? Are you suggesting that I do this all the time?"

"I'm suggesting that you're not doing it to do damage to the building but to do damage to your foot."

Brian appeared shocked. "Why would I want to do damage to my foot? I'm an athlete. Without my foot, I'm nothing. I lose my scholarship."

"But what if you didn't get caught and you only made non-damaging cuts on your foot; would you lose your scholarship then?"

"Not if it didn't interfere with my ability to wrestle, run, or lift."

"So it might be important to continue to kick in windows? Does it hurt when the glass cuts your foot?"

"Yeah, it hurts."

"Is that good? Do you seek that pain?"

"You're making me sound crazy."

I wondered whether Brian was jealous of the wealthier kids and perhaps concerned about his future.

"Your GPA doesn't suggest that you're going to graduate school easily, anyway. What happens to you next year?"

"I don't know!" He became tearful. "A lot of the other guys have parents who will set them up in businesses of their own or get them jobs with big-deal companies they know the owners of. You're right. I have nowhere to go next year. I am tough; okay-looking, I guess. I'm in pretty good shape, but that doesn't cut it after graduation. This May is like a cliff I'm going to fall off, into nowhere."

"Is that why you're cutting your foot, kicking in windows? I think that it solves a lot of problems for you. It takes care of your anger about the unfairness of life, and the pain and blood distract you from thinking about the future, and prove to you that you can take whatever 'pain' life will throw at you after graduation. You're good at taking pain, aren't you?"

All six foot four inches of this trim but very muscular young man shook with sobs.

"Yeah, I'm good at taking pain! I need it, so I never forget to be prepared when it's coming. And it's gonna come. Because next year I'm going to be nothing! I could come back here for a few days in September and relive who I used to be. But it's really over for me. College was a setup. I couldn't get higher grades if I wanted to. I'm one of the biggest, strongest, but definitely *not* the smartest, not even smart enough to be here."

I picked up his foot and put it on my knees to look at it. "Looks like you've done this at least six times. Maybe we should find a better way to get rid of the 'cliff' waiting for you in May."

Brian and I met regularly for the rest of the school year. He told me about the old movies he had watched with his dad while growing up in Massachusetts in a former factory town. His father, a man toughened by years of physical labor, loved John Wayne movies; as they watched, he would often exclaim to his son, "You've got to bite the bullet! That's a real man, a hero—no whimpering and whining when *he* gets hurt!"

Many of Brian's friends had tattoos, earrings, and other piercings. Among the athletes it was as important to brag about how much it hurt as it was to brag about their sexual exploits. Acceptance of pain was deemed bravery among the young men, just as it had been by his father.

Earlier, I stated that in most cases one does not begin with a culturally acceptable, "healthy" behavior, and cross over the line to what we call "psychopathological," yet in Brian's case this is what happened. Brian had to prove to himself that he was manly enough to survive life's pain without flinching. His own feelings of anxiety were threatening to pierce the tough facade, so, rather than lose his heroic self-image, he used his tolerance of pain to keep it together.

In therapy, Brian learned that he could express his feelings verbally instead of having to "bite the bullet." Given the opportunity to share his fears about his future, he was able to calm down, stop cutting himself, and develop a reasonable plan that included summer school, a part-time job, and financial aid toward a master's in physical therapy.

When self-mutilation has its beginnings in what is culturally acceptable, as it did with Brian, and can be interfered with by treatment early on, the outlook is better than if the self-mutilating behavior is truly an invention of the individual, devoid of societal origins. In the first case, the individual can consciously trace the roots of this behavior to something of which he is aware, rather than having to probe the unconscious deeply to find out what the behavior symbolizes. When the self-mutilation is more seriously hidden from the individual, it usually represents the "glue" that holds a fragile personality organization together.

Unfortunately for young people like Shari and Brian, culturally approved pain has a place and a presence in our society. It will always be with us in one form or another. As long as competition and heroic tasks exist, bravery, danger, and pain will exist in tandem, side by side. We must be vigilant, however, lest we as a society go overboard in confusing achievement with, and conferring status on, the endurance of pain.

10

THE FAMILY SYSTEM

When does a breakdown in family communication lead a child to self-sabotage? When does family discord manifest itself in one or more of the children, in forms ranging from under-achievement to lethal self-harming behavior? In this chapter, I want to establish a causal relationship between the degree of provocative behavior on the part of parents—or siblings and other powerful figures—and the resulting self-harming behavior in a child. The parental relationship proves to be a major influence in fostering such harmful behavior. A second major element is the deficit, or shortage, of genuine communication between other family members and the self-harming child.

We are all aware that there is no such thing as the perfect fam-ily. What we are concerned with here is that gray area where the imperfection becomes dangerous to the mental and emotional de-velopment of a family member. It is at that point, when psy-chopathological symptoms begin to appear in one member, that we want to evaluate and adjust the ways in which all the family members relate to each other. Then the newly appearing symptoms will lose the fuel that drives them.

Pitfalls in Family Life

In most reasonably healthy families, parents are the prime influences on the family structure. If, on the contrary, a child is directing the family system, parents need to reorganize the situation immediately.

When we talk about revising the family system, we are not talking about blame. The assumption here is that everyone is doing the best they can. Parenting style is not the measure of one's soul, nor of the depth of one's love for one's child.

Parenting style can be affected, or impaired, by a number of vulnerabilities, of which the following are most common:

- Financial stress
- Employment or unemployment stress
- Chronic illness or disability
- Emotional disorders, most commonly depression
- Alcoholism
- Drug abuse
- Marital incompatibility
- Divorce
- Death of a spouse

Each of these situations (possibly others) usually has an adverse effect on the development of at least one child in the family.

FINANCIAL AND EMPLOYMENT STRESS

When parents have to choose financial priorities that may deprive one member of the family in favor of another (e.g., one child gets to go to college and one doesn't), guilt and stress infiltrate almost every communication between the two children. This may cause strife between the parents as well. When a parent feels guilty toward a child, after a period of time, the child is perceived as the source of the parent's guilt and becomes someone to be angry at.

The child who is sensitive to this anger may internalize it and blame herself for her parent's unhappiness, even though she is the one who lost out in preferential treatment. The child who has benefitted from the decision, in turn, will be acutely aware of any punishing behavior the other child is receiving, and blame herself for having "caused" the situation. This acceptance of blame could lay the groundwork for either child to begin to inflict harm on herself.

Employment or unemployment stress can create numerous money-based problems. These are not the only ramifications of a precarious financial situation, however. Feeling insecure about one's ability to support a family is a demoralizing experience for a parent. Fear of his or her potential incompetence severely undermines a parent's confidence. The parent will resent being made to feel so devalued, and at the same time feel both angry at and intimidated by his or her own children. If this intimidation is communicated to a child, it can prematurely empower her, or even push her into the role of parent.

Parents under such stress may look to their own child for reassurance, emotional support, even validation. Those who are especially vulnerable to this parent-child **role reversal** are people whose own parents were harsh or critical. Seeking the unconditional love they lacked in childhood, these parents unwittingly place their child in a position of emotional authority: she becomes the family decision maker.

When the child in turn experiences herself as more powerful than her parents, she has no source of security. The child with no authority figures to lean on may invent behaviors that become very important to her, since she desperately needs something to depend on. She invents a system of ideas and behaviors that are immature and simplistic, reflecting the lack of guidance from a mature adult. In order to sustain herself emotionally, she makes self-inflicted pain a dependable and necessary part of her life.

We call such pervasive and needfully executed behaviors **rituals**. They range from obsessive-compulsive rituals to the ritualized regime of eating disorders to ritualized self-harming behaviors.

CHRONIC ILLNESS OR DISABILITY

Chronically ill or depressed parents can also leave an authority, or security, vacuum, which is difficult to fill. If we are talking about a married couple, the nondisabled parent may be overwhelmed with the burden of caring for the disabled parent at the same time he or she is earning a living to support the family. This is another type of situation that invites quick loss of temper, or emotional withdrawal, on the part of the overburdened parent. Either parent in such a situation may become frustrated and abusive toward a particular child. Such abusive behavior can intensify until it becomes a regularly occurring, severe event.

It is then only a short step for the child to take over the punishment she is receiving and become her own punisher. This may be done out of guilt or actually out of a need for the "soothing pain" originally created by the parent and then recreated by the child when she is lonely, because "pain" has begun to mean "home"—a recurring equation among self-mutilators. As we have seen, some children who are the victims of parental abuse (whether emotional or physical) learn to embrace pain because it is intermingled with whatever bits of love, nurturance, or attention they have ever received.

EMOTIONAL DISORDERS

When a parent suffers from an emotional disorder—the statistically most common being depression—that person usually stops functioning as an active parent, often becoming withdrawn and passive about child care and supervision. This rarely leads to the kind of aggressive behavior mentioned earlier. It *does* lead to anger on the child's part, against the depressed parent for failing that child.

Such anger is usually suppressed by the child, however, since she is also aware that the parent she is angry at is deemed helpless to overcome his or her depression. If this suppressed anger becomes too much for her to cope with, and she lacks a sympathetic and understanding audience, the child may begin to hurt herself out of the intensity of her frustrations, which have no other outlet.

ALCOHOLISM

Alcoholism poses an additional threat to the children of its sufferers beyond that of chronic mental illness. The alcoholic parent, while drinking, is more likely to commit physical abuse and even sexual abuse against one or more children than a parent who is not an alcoholic. This creates the dual problem for the child of, first, seeing her family in chaos and danger, and second, fearing for her own safety.

If the drinking and violence persist over years, the child may fight off feelings of helplessness by accepting the abuse and adjusting to it as if it were normal. She may become grandiose and believe that it is up to her to stop or limit the violence of the drinker. At this point, she may have become so inured to the abuse that she sees it as part of her relationship with the alcoholic parent. When this occurs, she simply expects the abuse, and it is fused with her general relationship with the parent. For her to abuse herself then is merely to do what she has been taught to think of as a normal experience.

The child has enough perspective, however, to know that this kind of behavior is something that cannot be shared with others. She is ashamed at being hurt by her alcoholic parent, and just as ashamed at her need to hurt herself, even if she doesn't understand why she is doing it.

DRUG ABUSE

When a parent suffers from drug addiction—cocaine, for example—he or she experiences the angry edginess that most cocaine addicts endure, in addition to the distancing and numbing effects of the drug. This combination makes a parent short-tempered, even violent, as well as emotionally unavailable to the child. But no matter what the drug is, if the parent is truly an addict, the mood swings that the child is exposed to are so severe that she will soon become aware that her parent is under the influence of a drug and see that parent as a person of no resource for her.

Again, as with the child of an alcoholic, she might see herself as the only one who can minimize the parent's drug usage. If a child sets these types of expectations for herself, they can only lead to disappointment and, sometimes, a reversal of the parent-child authority-dependence relationship, as we saw with the case of parents with financial or employment problems.

At times the child will be aware of the parent's extreme edginess, restlessness, agitation, and hostility—when the parent is "strung out," or going through withdrawal and in need of the drug. During these periods, the child may be victimized and harmed in a variety of ways by the parent. Like the child of the alcoholic parent, the child of the drug-addicted parent finds such abuse "normal" within the context of this sick relationship, and, again, she could very well "apply" the parental abuse to herself without the parent being there. This behavior could be termed **role-modeled** behavior. While it may be hard to see self-mutilation as role-modeled behavior, the self-mutilator who is receiving such pain can, in some cases, unconsciously reconnect with her parent.

MARITAL INCOMPATIBILITY: CAUGHT IN THE MIDDLE

When parents are strongly incompatible with each other, this incompatibility, which is characterized by a lack of communication between the couple, can also spread to the children, and usually

does. Or the incompatibility may take the form of aggression between the parents, and the child is caught in the middle. The child
may also become **triangulated**, or mistargeted, by one of the
parents, receiving the aggression meant for the other parent. Again,
if the pattern repeats itself, the child who is the recipient of the aggression sees her own absorption of the abusive behavior as helping to hold the family together.

In her reframing of the meaning of her being abused, the child
sees acceptance of the abuse as noble and constructive. In later
years she may even perpetuate the abuse with the unconscious intention of "creating harmony."

DIVORCE

Children of divorced parents are often faced with needy, angry, and
jealous parents, who rival one another over their child's affection.
As young children recover from the marital disintegration, they
may take advantage of this to get their way by playing one parent's
needs against the other. Parents are vulnerable to the child's manipulation because of their insecurity, and their anxiety. They may
transfer their anger toward the ex-spouse to the child, accusing the
child of possessing character traits of the disliked former spouse.

That child will believe the parent's accusations. It is too difficult
for children to disbelieve a parent, which is the emotional equivalent of losing the parent entirely.

DEATH

The child of a widowed parent may be the child of a needy parent. The child of one parent rarely argues with her only parent because she does not have an alternate parent to move toward. If
there is a relationship problem, the precious sole parent must not
be damaged or alienated.

Any child of a single parent lacks the luxury of acting out, or
expressing anger, where it could damage the sole parent or the relationship with that only parent. If that parent is abusive and needy

at the same time, and child will be trapped between her role as the receiver of abusive behavior and abandonment by weakening the only parental tie she has.

Each of these situations saps parental energy, patience, the ability to make clear decisions, and the ability to offer nurturing in the form of affection, listening time, and reassurance to an anxious, angry, or confused child.

In addition, each of these situations may cause parents to be neglectful, irritable, impatient, angry, rageful, and verbally or physically abusive, as a reaction to their own depletion and stress.

You Can't Choose Your Parents

A child who experiences any manifestation of parental stress, stemming from any of the situations just described, may choose self-harming or self-mutilating behavior as the expression of her overwhelming need to release negative feelings without hurting anyone else. The reason for choosing oneself as the target is the fear that one's parents cannot tolerate the anger without being damaged further. In addition, the child fears a loss of love for verbally expressing her anger.

A second, even less healthy reason for self-mutilating behavior is that the chronic infliction of any of the above aggressive parental behaviors against a child will cause the child to fuse **love-attachment-abuse** into a single complex cluster of feelings. If a parent physically abuses the child while verbally declaring love or care, the child's desire for attachment becomes the glue that fuses these two contradictory messages. This will result in the self-infliction of pain as a way of dealing with loneliness and the need for parental companionship.

The most common dynamic of self-mutilation occurs in the first example: that of an adolescent acting out against herself as a compensatory or substitute release against the parent. Ironically, these acts are most frequently committed by the more nurturing, understanding children, who can't bring themselves to risk hurting or harming their parents.

Let's see how this operated for Juanita, the youngest child and scapegoat of the family who emigrated from Mexico (chapter 2). When Juanita was abused or disapproved of by her family, she could act out against herself with a vengeance, using a knife or scissors. Even her cutting had an intense energy to it and often produced deep cuts and broad scars. The timing of her cutting was a clue to its unconscious motivation. It would take place either after a dispute with her parents—whether in person or on the telephone—or after a long period of no contact with them, which she inferred was their excluding her from the family.

Annika, whom we met in chapter 1, discovered that physical pain was an antidote for generalized anxiety. "It wasn't pain I was feeling, it was like an injection of Novocaine that the dentist uses; it makes pain go away even though the needle 'pricks' as the dentist puts it in. And because I controlled the pain, there was no fear with it."

For Annika, her cutting was a calming remedy for her feelings of emotional discomfort. She turned the disturbing behavior into something soothing for herself. To understand her reasons for doing this, we must backtrack and take a look at her history.

The Nurturance Vacuum

Annika's mother was left by her father for another woman when Annika was eight years old. Her father, a moderate alcoholic, re-married a recovered alcoholic. Annika's father would often call her late at night to talk to her. He asked about her in an obligatory style: "Are you okay? Is everything all right?" She sensed that she was supposed to answer, "Yes."

He promptly went on to tell Annika how her mother was asking for too much money from him for child support and what a tough time he was having getting his life started with his new wife. He always sounded so wretched that Annika didn't consider the possibility of confronting him about how inappropriate it was for him to complain to her about her mother. In this way the father was unconsciously making Annika responsible for her own child support, especially when he voiced complaints about her mother, who was hassling him for more money.

While all this was going on at least twice a week, Annika watched her mother become increasingly depressed over being abandoned by her husband for another woman. The mother complained repeatedly about the financial difficulties they were having because Annika's father would not give them enough money.

Annika saw a needy parent no matter which way she thought of turning for support. On some level she understood that her welfare was not uppermost in either of her parent's minds. Yet her anger toward them for trapping her in the middle was repressed and hard for her to identify.

"I think that they're both doing the best they can, but they just can't offer me any support because they're both drowning."

"Is there anyone you can turn to for support?" I asked.

"No. They are both only children and their parents are all dead. So I have no other family. I often wish that I had never been born. I miss the way it was before they started arguing, or at least before I knew they were unhappy with each other. I miss feeling like they were my mommy and daddy. I guess that's gone forever. Now I feel like I'm an orphan with two children—them."

Annika was not feeling the thwarted rage that Juanita experienced. She was not looking for a way to vent anger and settle for using her own body for that purpose. But she ended up using the same behavior as Juanita because the experience of cutting herself took her away from the inescapable trap of her neediness, ignored by her parents since they were both "drowning" in their own problems. Annika described her feelings before cutting herself as "lonely, nostalgic, sad." Then she would nearly "disappear" into a semi-trancelike state, and begin the cutting.

"It just takes me away from my life." She shrugged her shoulders sadly.

Annika's cutting had not become more severe, more endangering, but it did become more frequent, as did her trancelike states. These trance states were seen by her friends, though somehow she kept the actual cutting unobserved by anyone.

Then one day she was helping her mother in the kitchen and in the blink of an eye she cut quickly and deeply into her wrist while her mother had her back to her, scrubbing vegetables in the sink. The running water and the humming microwave concealed the sounds of Annika slipping to the floor. It was probably a minute or two before her mother turned around to see her daughter lying on the floor in an expanding puddle of blood.

Annika was rushed by ambulance to a nearby hospital. She had lost nearly two units of blood and was in danger of going into shock. In addition to severing the veins in her wrist, she had cut several nerves and tendons. She would need emergency microsurgery in order to allow her eventually to use her hand again. Doctors and psychiatrists interviewed her to determine if she was attempting to kill herself.

Annika was surprised at the commotion that she had created. "Do you know that you almost died?" one nurse said. Annika told the doctors that she had no intention of jeopardizing her life, or her hand, for that matter. She explained that the reason the cut was so deep was because she made it in a hurry. She hadn't wanted her mother to see her doing it. She planned to tell her mother that it was an accident that happened while she was quartering the chicken. She then showed the hospital staff all the other smaller cuts on her forearm and explained that she did this frequently when she got upset.

For the first time she was eager to show her handiwork to

others, as testimony that she wasn't trying to kill herself. She had a routine behavior that never in the past produced harm, other than small scars.

The hospital staff was in a quandary. Annika's action fulfilled all the criteria for a serious suicide attempt, but her explanations and her manner were not those of a suicide attempter who had been thwarted. The staff kept her in the hospital for nearly a week until the surgery had healed enough for her to go home. But they insisted that as part of her discharge plan she must enter regular psychotherapy because of her "routine," as she called it, of cutting herself.

Earlier, I stated that Annika's cutting had become more frequent. This was not due to an increase of stress from intensified parental pressure, but rather to her anticipating the next demanding conversation with either of her parents. Individuals who encounter periodic stress or difficulties of the same sort learn to anticipate them. Since these experiences were usually accompanied by anxiety, we refer to this as **anticipatory anxiety**. In the case of the cutter, she will often react to anticipatory anxiety with **anticipatory cutting**. Hence, Annika increased the frequency of her cutting to a point where if she thought that she might have to have a "heart-to-heart" talk with either parent, she would cut herself before and after the talk.

During Annika's third therapy session in the hospital, she gazed at her bandaged hand, resting in its supportive sling, then looked up at me and said wearily, "It will be a year before they even know if the nerves in my hand will ever work again. The stuff I did to protect me from my life may make me a cripple for life. Will it ever stop getting worse?"

Annika's original provocation for cutting herself was unfortunately commonplace: Her parents got divorced. After they divorced, they fell into the patterns that so many divorced parents do. Fearing the loss of love from their child, they compete for the child in a dependent style. To make matters worse, there were the elements of alcoholism. Nevertheless, this is a typical situation except that it contributed to a very serious, even life-endangering psychological disorder. In Annika's case, I am sure that the hereditary link to her father's alcoholism also tipped the scales toward this disorder.

———

In examining the backgrounds of cutters and other self-mutilators, we see a range of family situations and changes that runs from relatively benign to insensitive, abusive, and cruel. In juxtaposition, we see self-mutilating behaviors that range from repetitive—often at a minor level—to uneven in their endangering ability to lethal. In most cases, with the exception of incest (which causes the most catastrophic consequences), there is little relationship between the level of family dysfunction and provocation and the dangerousness of the self-mutilator's behavior.

Obviously, other elements are at work beyond the family structure. These include chemical hereditary factors, the presence of other disorders, and social components.

Parents who are concerned that a child may be at risk for self-mutilation can take the following precautions:

—develop their ability to be patient with the child's feelings;
—provide time for the child to discuss problems or worries;
—be consistent in providing verbal reassurance and security;
—practice communication between the couple about their child;
—avoid role reversal (letting the child become the parent) by being calmly authoritative; and
—offer positive models of self-worth, conflict resolution, and flexibility.

11

INCEST AND OTHER CHILDHOOD ABUSE: FUSING PAIN WITH SECURITY

How can the unspeakable experience of incest or other child-hood abuse, committed by someone familiar to or related by blood to a child, result in a desire on the child's part to recreate the pain humiliation, and isolation experienced? Here we will see how emotional pain can resurface in the victims of such abuse in the disguised form of self-mutilation.

Taking the Bad with the Good

Common sense suggests that if we have experienced something frightening, painful, humiliating, or destabilizing, we will try to avoid such negative experiences in the future at all costs.

Why, then, do some victims of sexual, physical, and emotional abuse "return to the scene of the crime" committed against them, again and again? Previously we have examined the concept of the "fusing of incompatible feelings," the paradox—though contrary to common sense—which describes the fusing of the desires to be loved and punished or harmed by the same person.

We have all heard the expression, "You have to take the bad with the good." We understand this to mean that in life, one's expectations may not take into consideration the trials and tribulations that come our way. What we all expect, however, from this mixture is that on balance, the good will outweigh the bad.

How do we apply such a tried-and-true principle to individuals who seem to seek out situations where the bad clearly outweighs the good?

A child who is abused tries to see the abuse as a form of love, attention, or some other valuable attachment, in order to make the abuse tolerable at the time of original occurrence. This not only causes her to overlook the painful experience her abuser is inflicting upon her but also to fail to distinguish between the abuse and the benefits in the relationship. They are all fused together into one relationship, one experience. She literally takes the "good" and the "bad" as a blending, a compound, and accepts them as one experience with two components that are inseparable. As she becomes deeply involved in this **valued-abuseive relationship**, she even learns to distrust kind behavior if it doesn't include abusive elements. Here we see the powerful influence of early development.

Emmy: When Harm and Help Collide

Emmy was the youngest of three children, the daughter of a prominent general surgeon in a small city in the Midwest. Emmy's father was regarded as a community hero due to his medical ability to save lives in the emergency room and in cardiac bypass surgery. Emmy grew up in a time and a place where medical specialists were a luxury that this city and the hospital couldn't afford. She was well aware that her father was regarded as special, good, and powerful by her community. He was the one who set her broken arm when she fell off her bicycle at five. He was also the man who raped her in the middle of the night that same year, telling her to "be a big girl and don't cry." He warned her not to tell her mother or anyone else.

"Virgil," as Emmy referred to her father, repeated this behavior two or three times a week until she was twelve years old. During these years he taught her sailing, fly-fishing, horseback riding, and ornithology. He taught her methodically and patiently, and she excelled in all of these activities. She was nearly always present when the city bestowed various awards on her father. He was present when she received an award for her ornithology project, and another for her "junior sailing skills."

In public, she always addressed him as "Dr. Whitelaw," never "Daddy," though occasionally "Father" at large family dinners.

When her father "completed" his sexual act, which Emmy experienced as painful and nearly suffocating, due to his enormous size in contrast to her small body, he left her room and closed the door. She immediately forgot the episode.

In fact, Emmy forgot all of these events. She only began to remember them in her late twenties, after her marriage failed and her husband left her. Her husband said that he always felt that she was coldly and reluctantly submissive when he wanted to be romantic or sexual. "I'm tired of you doing me favors. I'm tired of feeling like a beggar sexually."

She describes her husband as a warm person, who she was sure would always be gentle. He was, and she felt little, if any, passion with him. She did care for him very much, though, and his leaving brought her to such a state of incapacity that she could barely take care of their two children.

It was several months after he left her that Emmy started having dreams of being pursued by a "giant of a man." "He began to look more and more like my father. In my dreams, he caught me. Each dream brought back more details until I realized that they were not symbolic of anything but actual events I was not ready to remember when I was awake. I finally sat down and wrote them all out, remembering them as events, not dreams. That's when I decided to enter therapy."

Emmy didn't dare "remember" her experiences during childhood. If she had, it would have meant losing the positive side of her relationship with her father, all the things they did together, the protection of his community's esteem, and his daytime vigilance when he could take care of any injury that might befall her. Somehow she made an unconscious decision that the "good" outweighed the "bad."

Her adolescence was punctuated by romances with boys from the "wrong side of the tracks" whom her father objected to strenuously though she kept most of them a secret. She was the object of abuse in each of her relationships with these angry young men. But she always told them that if they ever hit her in the face, she would leave them. She was pushed, punched, shoved into walls, verbally abused, and raped. When the boys weren't abusing her, they were apologetic, guilty, sad, tender, loving, and gallant.

The damage from these abuses was as invisible as her father's rapes had been. Most importantly, Emmy felt that these relationships were normal. She was quite attracted to these boys; there were, in fact, four separate romances in sequence. One for each year of high school. She explained that she found these boys the most exciting and arousing of all who pursued her.

Emmy came to her first session with her diary notes in hand. Her manner was matter-of-fact, her dress seductive. Her skirt was shorter than most. It kept getting shorter during the interview as she slid down the seat of the chair, readjusted her position, then repeated the action. Her blouse was unbuttoned to the point of indiscretion, and she leaned over in my direction every time she referred to her notes about her dreams and memories.

"Are you dating men now?" I asked her.

"Well, it's been a year since Tom left me. I think that it's about

time I moved on with my life, although I still miss him and probably always will."

She showed a momentary sadness when speaking about Tom.
She was wearing a shiny pink silk blouse with long sleeves and
french cuffs, and large cufflinks—gold squares with big pearls in
the center.

I commented, "Your cufflinks are pretty, feminine and large.
They almost suggest 'locks' at the ends of your sleeves."

She looked at me cautiously, then said, "Yes, they are locks. The
boyfriends I had in high school were not allowed to harm my face.
That would give it all away—that I was getting beaten. They were
not the only ones who were allowed to harm me. *I* am also allowed to harm myself. Since I have told you everything else, I
might as well tell all, as they say."

With that she undid one of her massive cufflinks and rolled up
the broad sleeve almost to her shoulder, to reveal dozens of small
to medium cuts on her lower and upper arm. She then proceeded
to undo the other cufflink—her right—and rolled up that sleeve
to reveal fewer but much larger cuts, and laceration scars running
two inches long and quite broad. Some of them were still pink and
angry-looking.

"I should really keep two cufflinks on the right sleeve. I don't
own *any* short-sleeve blouses. I would buy long-sleeve bras if they
sold them." The seductive smile returned.

"I find it interesting and contradictory that you are so careful to
cover up your scars of self-abuse when at the same time you carefully uncover your thighs and breasts to socially acceptable limits
and perhaps a bit beyond. Do you think that there is any connection between these contrasting behaviors?"

She quickly pulled her skirt hem down and buttoned a button
on her blouse. She looked up at me, crossed her legs, and began to
cry. The seductive look and tone were gone.

"I guess there are two Emmys inside of me. If I show you both at once, I 'short out.' I *had* to show you both at once. Anyway, you knew. Your comment about my cufflinks was a giveaway.

"I don't think that they, those two Emmys, are really in contrast with each other," she went on. "I think they are each half of me. If I lost either half I might disintegrate, like the witch in *The Wizard of Oz* when Dorothy poured water on her. You know, I only cut myself when I am not involved with a man. I started cutting myself when 'Dr. Whitelaw' went away on lecture tours. He could be gone for a week at a time. In the light of what I remember now, you'd think I would be happy and take the best care of my body when he wasn't around to hurt it. I guess I must have always been crazy, because when *he* didn't hurt me, I did. Why?"

I waited a minute or so for her to hear what she had just said. "Maybe everything he did *with* you and *to* you were integral parts of one relationship. When he was away, you might have gone bird-watching. That was something you did with him. Instead, you evoked pain and damage to yourself. That was something else that he did to you. The pain and damage were a stronger reminder of him than the pleasant things you did together. It was also your secret, for better or worse. That combination made hurting yourself a way of feeling closer to him. Despite the monstrous things he did to you, those things registered as 'fathering' just as the nice things did.

"Children cannot really judge their parents, as parents. They are in no position to decide that they're being parented by evil-doers, or incompetents. If they were to make that decision, they would be erasing the feeling that they had parents. They would experience a 'separation anxiety' more painful than all the harmful deeds done to them by their parents. So they choose to side with their parents, warts and all."

"So does that mean I'm crazy?" she demanded. "You were right. I was 'flashing' you like I do with all men, whether I like them or not. You see both sides of me. Will I have to be like this the rest of my life? Will I have to keep seducing men and alternately cutting myself? I'm thirty-two years old. I'm intelligent. I have a college degree and two graduate degrees. Shouldn't I know better? *He* can't come into my bedroom to rape me anymore. Am I addicted to that, or something that resembles that?"

Emmy was "addicted to that," as she put it, because it was a powerful part of her formative years' development. That didn't mean that she would have to remain attached to the terrible triad of seduction–rape–self-mutilation. But it would take years of therapy to undo the damage done during her formative years. I explained this to her.

"How can that damage be undone?" she asked.

"When you came in here, you did your characteristic behavior; your formative years' learning was guiding you. I did not respond to reinforce it, and now you aren't behaving that way at all with me. That will have to happen over and over for you to learn new behaviors and responses to replace your childhood learning, and you will need a very constant and consistent person to play it off against—your therapist."

She looked startled and suspicious. "I can see that therapy will make me feel vulnerable, self-conscious, embarrassed. And when you pointed out my flashing you, it made me feel like a whore. What if I can't take it . . . this therapy?"

"Do you feel embarrassed now? Do you feel like a whore now?"

"No."

"Then it was a painful, though brief moment for you?"

"I guess so."

"Then I guess that you *can* take it."

She smiled, relieved. "I guess you're right. This is weird, talking to you like this. I never have talked to anyone like this before."

"So the upside of this risky experience which could make you feel all the 'bad' feelings you just mentioned is that it could also make you feel some 'safe' feelings that are new to you?"

She nodded.

I knew that the most difficult task we had ahead involved the deconstruction of the part of her personality that had aligned her self-abuse, the cutting, with the abuse she elicits from the men she becomes involved with, and the rapes that she experienced from her father.

"You mean, no more cutting—no more raping?"

"It does sound strange that I'm asking you to give up seeking what most people would regard as a living hell."

I noticed that Emmy took a certain pleasure in deliberately using the word "raping," referring to her own experience in being the victim of acts that people normally describe with reluctance and hesitation. I thought that she had been wanting to tell on her father for a long time, and in the privacy of the therapy office, she was paradoxically "shouting it from the rooftops."

She was more comfortable talking about the rapes than her cutting. She could express her righteous rage at what was done to her by another. She was ashamed at what she had done to herself.

"I wonder how long it will take you to remove the 'locks' from your sleeves?" I commented at the end of our session.

She looked down at the massive cufflinks, stared at them for a moment, and without looking up, shrugged her shoulders. Tears splashed on her blouse.

She finally looked up at me. "I guess, for some weird reason, I would rather tell the world on my father than what's under my sleeves."

"I guess that you're more confident about the assaults being over than you are about your ability to stop assaulting yourself. I think that when you told me about them, for the first time you realized that they were more than your secret. They were also your shame."

"Yeah, that was a real surprise to me."

"Perhaps we can weave a lot of surprises together that will become the fabric of your recovery."

"I hope so," she responded with an optimistic nod.

"I *am* going to ask you to 'unlock' your sleeves at each session, in the future, you know?"

She drew a long breath. "Yeah, I guess you better do that."

Emmy has been in therapy for three years now. The work has had three major focuses:

- Examining how she was affected by what her father did to her at the time it was happening, when it stopped, and in the present.
- Examining her relationships with men, including how she coped with me as a male therapist.
- Reducing and eventually eliminating her need to use cutting herself as a substitute for communicating mental and emotional pain.

Future sessions will involve her relationships with other women, including her anger toward her mother; her first anger after realizing what had been happening; her making a positive adjustment to her sexual arousal; and her ability to eliminate self-hate when it occurs, and to feel as if it belongs to her, not her abusers. If and when she becomes involved in a romantic relationship, these issues will have to be reexamined to check her progress so that her past doesn't distort or sabotage the relationship.

Emmy's inability to remember the assaults she experienced from her father was necessary until enough time had passed and she was far enough away from his power over her. This "power" also included the opportunity for him to offset the assaults with positive and protective behaviors that were part of his relationship with her. These positive acts on his part were valuable to Emmy and to lose them would cause her to lose whatever self-esteem she had. Her father had come to symbolize that fusion of security, pain, and humiliation discussed earlier in this chapter. If he would not be the source of her pain, then she would become the source of her own pain. This would simultaneously produce a sense of security as well.

The "filing system" Emmy had developed of using her left arm for the 'lesser' pains, and smaller cuts, and her right arm for the greater pain and the larger cuts developed over the length of time since she first began cutting. She didn't want to make one cut over another; this would diminish the statement made by the earlier cut. She simply ran out of room on her left arm. She also developed a need for greater pain and damage to herself as she became used to the threshold of pain she was creating.

Emmy stopped cutting herself after the first eighteen months in treatment and hasn't cut herself for the past year and a half. The other treatment issues will take longer to resolve since they involve personality reconstruction and building skills of relating emotionally that didn't exist before. Her family system hadn't allowed them to develop.

Loretta: How Bad Becomes Good

Nonincestuous emotional, physical, and sexual abuse can produce a fusion of abuse, pain, and attachment similar to that produced by incest.

Loretta grew up in a family that reorganized several times. The first time occurred when her father left her mother when Loretta was five. He simply disappeared. Her mother stayed at home crying for the first year, then took a job with a computer company, where she met another man. After a brief courtship, they were married. Loretta's mother was needy, taking many medications, suffering from anxiety and depression. Nick found this damsel-in-distress just what he needed. She was pretty and she wanted someone who would "take command" of her life—and, unfortunately, Loretta's.

Nick would impose all sorts of rules and restrictions on Loretta. She had lots of chores to do and little time for herself. It was easy for Nick to convince his helpless wife that he was building character in his stepdaughter. When Loretta reached puberty, Nick noticed how boys and men looked at his thirteen-year-old stepdaughter and increased his restrictions on her free time. By now, however, she was becoming more resourceful at "escaping" for an hour here and there, especially during the day while Nick was at work. She discovered that boys at the nearby high school would treat her much better than her stepfather did. She found time both in and out of school to hang out with some of the more disreputable boys who were cutting classes and getting involved in gang violence, and violence in general.

At thirteen, Loretta looked three years older. The boys she became involved with wanted sexual activities that she wasn't ready for. But at the same time she didn't want to lose the physical and sexual affection that came with their compliments. She allowed herself to be mistreated by the older boys, who seemed to take pleasure in their mistreatment of her. She made the best of this situation by believing she had to put up with the bad to get the good. At home she didn't experience any "good" and there was plenty of "bad": Nick was critical of her, and she felt restricted in a loveless, noncaring environment. So if the "bad" she was putting up with from this gang of boys was more physical and sexual, the praise, even if it was crude, was worth it.

After a while, Loretta began to enjoy the sex play as well. It included physical exposure, embarrassment, and being treated roughly; smacked, hit, or cursed at by more than one boy at a time. When the boys grew tired of her, she developed the habit of picking at her face, which made her skin increasingly unattractive.

One day, fearing impending expulsion from the group, Loretta banged her head against the wall, and her reaction to the painful jolt it gave her was mixed. Later that week, when she was alone in one of the boy's houses, she took a fork and cut the back of her left hand with the last tine, which was bent slightly away from the others. She pressed hard and moved the tine slowly, pulling at the skin in its wake to cause the tine to penetrate more effectively. She made a small cut, a quarter-inch long, and stared at the droplets of blood that trickled across the back of her hand until the small stream fell between her middle and ring finger. She became so immersed in the process that it took away her fear of being abandoned by the boys. Loretta had found a way to drive away the fears of abandonment, loneliness, and emptiness so familiar to her at home and now amid these boys.

The boys eventually grew tired of her. The mainstream of students, labeling her a tramp, shunned her as well. She took to cutting herself with kitchen implements that she found at home. She enjoyed the irony of using objects that Nick had purchased, to cut herself. Occasionally, she would leave a little blood on one of them and watch his confusion over finding a paring knife with blood on it. Nick asked his wife whether she had cut herself using it. He never bothered to ask Loretta if she had cut herself. It was only when she made several cuts on her hand and was sent to the school nurse by a concerned gym teacher that all of this came out. She was then referred to a psychiatrist to determine if she was suicidal. He was unsure, but since he found so many small cuts on her hands, he diagnosed her as a "cutter," and referred her for therapy and medication.

Through cutting, Loretta became the master of her own pain. Cutting was better than the neglect and invisibility she experienced at home, from both her stepfather and her mother, who was too ill and needy to focus on her or his treatment of her. The boys mixed "appreciation" with their mistreatment of her, so that kind of pain was "part good," as she later explained. Like the incest victim, Loretta used self-inflicted pain to relieve her loneliness and emptiness. She had no faith in other people's ability to relieve these feelings for her.

When after two years in therapy (and medication for depression) she "realized" this connection, Loretta discontinued all self-harming behavior and began to work on her other ways of sabotaging her chances for social and academic success. At the same time her parents were seen as a couple, mandated by the county in order to avoid being designated neglectful parents, and they worked on improving positive communication with Loretta.

There are many possible reasons why a person can fuse pain with pleasure, perhaps not very different from those who fuse violence or inflict cruelty upon others with pleasure. People who make themselves their own target are more sympathetic to us, but arouse fear instead of anger within us. Most of us would not make ourselves the target of our own anger, nor would we use blood and pain to satisfy that anger, loneliness, and emptiness in this manner. Yet this is more common than we would like to believe, and heartbreaking to witness in someone we care about or love.

TOWARD

RECOVERY

12

A PERSPECTIVE

ON CHANGE

How many years does it take to develop the disorder of self-mutilation? How many years does it take to undo what has developed? The answers vary from person to person. When we examine the factors that influence the manifestation of self-mutilation in its victims, it is easy to see that time is integral to both the formation and the dissipation of these behaviors. This chapter will identify the kinds of energy, length of time, and styles of connecting with the patient required from those who would help her to change, both behaviorally and emotionally.

What are we trying to change? Again, the question must be posed differently for each person. The goal is to free the self-mutilator from physical, self-harming behaviors. These behaviors must continue to be monitored by the helper; lack of mention by the cutter can't be assumed to mean that the cutting is gone. Emotional distress, and areas of emotional and mental impediment to functioning in the world, must be discussed and made part of the goal of recovery.

In chapter 10, The Family System, we saw some of the circumstances that can plunge children into situations and thoughts upon which they can construct a world of ideas about themselves—what they "deserve" from others and life; how positively or negatively they should feel about themselves; and how they should treat themselves. If on balance such children develop negative ideas about themselves, through lack of spoken support by family members, they will believe that they deserve whatever negative behavior is directed toward them; not only will they accept that behavior but they will perpetuate it, and provoke it with family members and others, later on in life.

Familiar Ground

In individual psychotherapy, we want to change the expectations of the self-harming person by "depriving" them of negative and harmful verbal, or physical, responses from the therapist. Take, for example, a woman who had been a sexually abused child. In the middle of a session she suddenly proclaimed, "It's too hot in here," and took off her sweater, leaving her in a scanty bra. I reached for the afghan I usually keep on the side of the couch for my anorexia patients suffering from hypothermia, and draped it over her.

"There will be no abuse or sexual exploitation allowed you here," I said. Then, in a lighter tone, I added, "You may not be here just in your underwear." She became upset and embarrassed, put on her sweater, and left the session.

Several hours later she called me to apologize. I told her that I believed that she expected every male to want to exploit her because then she was on familiar ground. She said that was indeed the case, and that she didn't know what to do if that element was not a part of her relationship with a man. I explained that the absence of the abuse she had become accustomed to was confusing, but she would get used to it, and that I believed that if I deprived her of the abuse, she could learn how to deprive herself of cutting.

In this case, we are trying to change the expectations a self-harmer has for relationships that she developed *during her formative years,* which resulted in cutting herself, and sabotaging herself in many other ways. Here, individual psychotherapy is a long and arduous process for the patient. It can be sped up or shortened somewhat if family therapy is another component of treatment. The more significant people in her life who are involved in changing the patient's expectations, the more effective the treatment. In cases of verbal, physical, and sexual abuse by members of the family, apologies by the offender(s) are therapeutic, especially when they take some responsibility for their errors, removing as much self-blame as possible from the victim of this abuse.

Predictors of Recovery

The more people who are available as resources for treatment, the more powerful the treatment becomes. Again, what we are trying to fix are the self-destructive behaviors, the provocations sometimes initiated by the victim unconsciously, and the very nature of relationships that are being constructed in the present. We, of course, have to put the history of the individual in perspective for the self-harmer so she can better understand her own behavior. This is accomplished by an insight-oriented review of the individual's life.

There are many barometers we use to estimate how optimistic we can be about change; how much time that change will require; and how much change we can hope for.

These barometers are a function of

—The child's age when parental dependency, neglect, or abuse began.
—The frequency of each of the above.
—The severity of the misconduct in abusive cases or the intensity of the neediness of the parents in benign cases.

—The present support system of the individual: "Is life good enough to be worth getting better for?"
—Has the individual gone on to become seriously involved with a supportive person upon whom she can depend and trust?

These are only some of the ways we can estimate chances and degrees of a successful psychotherapeutic outcome. Other issues include hereditary-chemical factors and any additional psychiatric diagnoses and symptoms. Any other disorders present in the patient usually develop from the same core issues and can precede self-mutilation, which often develops *after* other diagnosed problems have emerged.

If a child first experiences neglect as an infant, she will adjust to the lack of attention, to not having her needs for holding, feeding, and being changed met, by lowering her expectations of care. Neglect results in depression at any point from infancy on. If a child is sexually hurt or stimulated by a caretaking figure, she (or he) will expect the same from all those in either caretaking or authoritative roles.

The infant or toddler is in no position to make moral judgments about these events, or her responses. It is only later on, toward puberty, that the child will sense the conflict between societal values regarding sexual behavior and her own early experiences. She will then be able to recognize that the neglect or abuse from a parent or caretaker is inappropriate. It is at this point that she will begin to devalue herself as someone who has accepted societal taboos. Her shame and lowered self-esteem will influence not only her relationships with others but how she relates to and manages her feelings about herself.

Here we need to reiterate the concept of a continuum from benign parental neglect—which consists of subtle messages of neediness, emotional exhaustion, or depletion—at one end of the scale all the way to the abusive behaviors I have described at the other extreme. It would be an error to assume that all self-mutilators come from families where cruelty and abuse are present.

We cannot change causes rooted in someone's past, but we can make changes in the present that will correct the need a person has to act out their characteristic symptoms, and so help to heal their negative self-image.

Influencing Change

There is a lot of advising and threatening on the part of family members and the health care profession, from physician to psychotherapist, as they try to influence the cutter to recover. Such threats and advice go unheeded by the cutter. The reason for this is the unwitting assumption of the adviser, or threatener, that he is talking to a reasonable person. A healthy personality responds positively to guidance, especially guidance that is highly consequential. In the case of the self-mutilator, we are not dealing with a healthy personality. The self-mutilator is not making choices with emotional freedom. Often she is not even aware of the actions she is taking; and when she is aware, she still feels *compelled, choiceless,* in the matter.

If advice, guidance, and threats are useless, what kind of communication is useful and will promote change? The prerequisite for the helper is to develop *influence* with the self-mutilator. Influence is not easy to come by with a person who has learned from her life experience to be wary of everyone—especially if they are in a position of authority or potential authority. This is particularly true for people who were the victims of abusive, pathogenic (illness-causing) behaviors and acts during their earliest development (from birth to two). This group is likely to find it the most difficult to recover. These are the ages when pain is readily fused with attachment, often resulting in psychotic episodes and severe personality disorders.

Ages three to nine are still powerful formative years, and when repeated pathogenic behaviors are directed toward a child during these years, no matter how subtle, that child makes an unhealthy adjustment to them that will emerge as both a personality disorder and a behavior disorder—the identified problem such as self-mutilation or anorexia that results in their being sent into therapy.

Though it is unusual, when abuses described in anecdotes are sporadic or highly infrequent—say, four times a year—the child is more likely to develop **phobias**, and **anticipatory anxiety attacks**, waiting for the abuse to be repeated the next time. This situation presents the least difficulty to treat and resolve. Note that I do not say it is "easy."

Patients Who Are More Difficult to Treat

Patients who have suffered from severe abusive or assaultive behavior will always be the most disturbed, most difficult to treat, requiring the longest treatment time (nearly a lifetime in some cases), and offering the poorest outlook for recovery. This is not to say that recovery is impossible, but it is very difficult.

In more benign situations, when parental neediness, expressed to a child, "drafts" that child into a caretaking position vis-á-vis her own parents, she is likely to feel resentful and deprived. A lack of supportive messages from her parents will lead to low self-esteem, with no way to redress her grievances. She cannot hurt the parents that she worries about and resents at the same time. So she will hurt herself. This kind of situation is characterized by the patient who feels she can't get angry at anyone but herself.

Some individuals come to treatment living lives that are devoid of support: their parents are ill or deceased, money is lacking, and there is not much hope of improving the situation due to lack of sufficient education and/or friends. This is one of those times where unless a plan is generated for the patient's life to improve, there isn't much incentive for her to overcome her problems and behaviors. One factor in this formula is whether or not the person can depend on someone else in her life—a lover, spouse, parent—who has become healthier since the patient was a child, to support and assist her recovery.

Neurological Impairments

In discussing psychological disorders, we cannot overlook certain other aspects that affect the development of the disorder, and the outcome for recovery. I am referring here to organic problems, which we classify as neurological impairments stemming from the improper functioning of neurotransmitters, most prominently, serotonin. If individuals do not have sufficiently active serotonin, they seem to suffer irritability, anxiety, and depression. If one adds to the provocations already listed insufficient serotonin activity in the brain, we have a heightened sensitivity to mental pain that will exacerbate all of the dynamics previously discussed.★ The implication of this organic problem is that certain individuals in treatment will require some form of antidepressant, sometimes coupled with a tranquilizer (benzodiazapine).

What we do not know at this time is whether "chemical" and "hereditary" forces are in fact the same. We do know that trauma during the formative years (and later) can affect the brain's chemistry, but at present there are no conclusive medical tests to evaluate a patient's need for medication. So, therapists look for the persistence of depression and anxiety. Medication is attempted by trial and error: a patient's response to medication becomes an indicator as to the need for it. Psychiatrists who specialize in medication (psychopharmacologists) are best equipped to make this assessment.

Another issue affecting outcome in treatment is the fact that self-mutilation is often the last symptom to appear in a chain of symptoms and diagnoses. Those that preceded its appearance are

★See Peter D. Kramer, *Listening to Prozac* (New York: Penguin Books, 1993).

significant. If a person is diagnosed as having a borderline personality disorder, the issues involved in improving or recovering from this condition are interwoven with treating the self-mutilation. The same is true for major depression, especially if it includes suicidal ideation (ideas). Other symptoms that often accompany the self-mutilating behavior may include substance abuse, eating disorders, anxiety disorders, and so on.

If we remember that self-mutilating behavior is a symptom for releasing discomfort, emotional pain, and other grievances, we need to realize that the self-harmer must learn other, healthier ways of expressing discomfort and emotional pain. *Talk, trust, healthy attachment, intimacy,* and *secure communication* are the necessary building blocks for change.

As we see that the roots of cutting, burning, and other forms of self-mutilation go deep and far back into a person's emotional history, we can understand that the amount of emotional energy the self-harmer will have to expend in order to change their characteristic self-destructive behavior is enormous. There is no question that the helper (whether therapist, friend, or family member) must be prepared to expend a fair amount of energy, skill, and knowledge in turn to provoke and facilitate that change.

1 3

REACHING OUT TO

REACH IN

How do we get a frightened, ashamed, guarded person to reveal herself to us? To make the task more difficult, she has not developed a language with which she can talk about herself. She has not grown up around others who permitted or role-modeled talk about their own feelings, their complexities, their conflicts in a manner that the child could hear, understand, and depend upon for support.

Typically, a self-harmer appearing in a therapist's office has nothing to say. She prohibits herself from complaining about others, or accusing them; to her, that's immoral. She can't complain about herself; that's being weak. She can't analyze or interpret what goes on inside her head, or between people she lives with, or peers she is friends with, because she has no vocabulary for this. She experiences her feelings of anger (when she *can* feel them) as dangerous.

More than likely the self-harmer sits down on a chair or

couch in a therapist's office and often presents a blank stare, waiting for the therapist to speak to her. She typically has been referred to the therapist. She often doesn't even know why she is
there.

Breaking the Ice

It can indeed feel as if there is no way to start the session that
won't sound chatty, patronizing, or worse, threatening. The way
around meeting someone who offers no invitation or opening
to converse is to keep in mind the description of her mental
state and outlook offered above. This will enable the therapist or
counselor to provide the generosity that the patient needs. It is
important that the therapist not have expectations for the patient
to talk much, if at all. This will be a long-term therapy because
its goal is to build up facets, communication skills, reflection
skills, into a personality riddled with deficits in these and other
areas.

The therapist, then, is the builder, the more active and sometimes the only active member of the pair.

Not all cutters present with such extreme communication
deficits as the **blank slate** patient, but perhaps it is best to start
with the most difficult. Other versions of the cutter are the **false
self**, who lacks genuineness, and says a lot, but nothing meaningful; and the **deflector**, who dodges every personal question by
telling an irrelevant story about someone else.

But let's return to our blank slate patient, who doesn't try to fool
or distract us, just offers us nothing to respond to. Well, not exactly
nothing. She presents an appearance in terms of body language,
and facial expressions, that is open for comment. Such comment
should focus upon unstated conflicts that her nonverbal communication suggests. Remember my earlier exchange with Emmy
(chapter 11) who wore the cufflinks.

The Silent Beginning

Fon arrived in the United States from Hong Kong when she was nine years old. Her father never sent for her mother. Shortly after his arrival, he married another woman. Fon was lost on Mott Street, bereft without her mother, and furious because of the new woman in her mother's place. She spoke only Cantonese up to that point and was enrolled in an elementary school in New York's Chinatown where she was teased by the first-generation native-born Chinese child, who called her "Foreigner" or *Ju kok*.

At home Fon was passively uncooperative; she did the dishes slowly, cleaned up after herself poorly. By the time she had reached seventh grade, she began to faint in the hallways during changes of class. She had to be carried to the school emergency room, where she would open her eyes but make no complaints about the way she felt. Her family was notified that she needed to go for a physical examination to determine the cause of these fainting episodes. They were afraid of government agencies, and the public school was considered allied with these agencies, so they complied.

On examination, Fon was given a clean bill of health, though bruises made with blunt instruments were found on the backs of both hands, her arms, and her legs. They were not serious, and the prevailing attitude at that time, twenty-five years ago, was that it was difficult for municipal services to enforce extensive cooperation from the Chinese community, which "took care of its own."

Fon was referred to me for school-based counseling. She came in to the office suffering from all the deficits mentioned above, as well as being limited in her ability to speak English. She had been in the United States for nearly three years but lived in a community where one was encouraged to speak Chinese outside of school.

Fon sat before me with a severely forlorn look on her face. She made strong eye contact with me but her eyes were set in a complex expression that I would have to call "angry defeat." Her lower lip protruded upward, raising her upper lip a bit. In her lap, clenched tightly with both hands, was a Chinese-English dictionary. She wanted to communicate. I kept my sentences simple.

"You look unhappy."

She stared away from me and tightened her face muscles.

"Now you look away. You don't want me to see your unhappiness."

She looked down at her dictionary.

"You want the book to talk to me about you."

She lifted the book several inches above her lap and subtly slammed it back down again.

"You are mad at the book."

She looked at me again. "I . . . am . . . mad . . . at . . . me! Myself is no good."

I argued, "You are alone."

Her eyes welled up. Several tears fell. "You see . . . no good! Good person not alone!" She nodded repeatedly.

I understood that her "no good" was her linguistic and culturally impaired way of saying volumes. I had to help her develop her ability to speak them, one page at a time.

I noticed black and blue marks on the back of her left hand. The doctor's notes had listed the bruises on both hands, suggesting abuse by another person. "What caused that?" I asked her, pointing to the back of her hand.

"Always there," she responded.

"No, that is not possible. That is caused by a blow." I hit the back of my left hand with my right. "Then it will go away, unless there is another blow."

"There is always another blow," she replied sourly.

"Why?"

"I told you, myself is no good. Hitting hand show that."

"Who hits your hand?"

She shrugged her shoulders, looking down. "Many people."

"Which people?"

"My father, my, um, stepmother. I hate her. I am mad at him. He not have to marry her."

"Who else hits you?"

"I hit me—harder than they can. Then I can be right."

"You are 'right' because you do to yourself what they do to you?"

She smiled and nodded defiantly.

"Why do you close your eyes and fall down?"

She looked surprised that I knew about the "fainting."

"I don't know why. Is good for me."

"It makes you feel good?"

"Everything goes away. I don't like when it's over. Everybody talk to me and ask me questions I don't know answer. Then everything bad is back in my head."

"What is in your head?"

"I don't know . . . but it bad, very bad, bad about me."

"You are sure that what is in your head is correct?"

She looked at me as if I had said something foolish.

"Of *course*—it is in my head. How not correct?"

"How do thoughts get into your head?"

She shrugged her shoulders, turning her palms out and up.

"I will tell you how thoughts get into your head." I raised my voice authoritatively, making intense eye contact and nodding my head for emphasis. She looked surprised but attentive as I continued.

"How did you learn words, to speak?"

"I don't know."

"When you were a baby, did people around you tell you the words? Did you hear the words from them? Did you learn the words from them?"

"Yes."

"If you grew up among silent people, people without talk, would you have words in your head?"

"I don't know."

"When you were a little girl in Hong Kong, were there English words in your head?"

"No."

"How did the English words get there?"

"English people put them there."

"Who put the Chinese words in your head?"

"Chinese people," she conceded.

"Which Chinese people?"

"My mother, my *real* mother, and my father."

"You copied the way they talked to you?"

"Yes."

"Did you copy what they said about you, and put that in your head?"

"Maybe"—she paused pensively—"but they are always right. They are my mother and father."

"The words in your head that tell you bad things about yourself, did you ever hear these words, these sentences from anyone else?"

"Yes, but they are correct. My parents could not say what is not correct even if I hate what they say. New mother is not true, but my father and real mother are true."

"What do these 'true' people say to you about yourself?"

"They say I'm bad girl."

"Tell me the sentences they use."

"They say, 'spoiled girl, ungrateful girl, girl should be sold to another family. Other family would own her, make her work harder.' I know nobody can like me, no good. See. I tell you before! If my parents cannot like me, only a fool can like me. Not true like. I am smart. I don't like me, too."

"You hit yourself, too. You fall down in the hallway. Where did you get the idea to fall down and close your eyes?"

"Sometimes I don't want to feel 'bad girl' ideas. I have to go away from myself."

At this point I was treading on dangerous ground. I was treating someone who grew up in a culture where parents are venerated, and I wanted to challenge what she had been taught by them. If I faced this task head-on, she would distrust me. I was, after all, a Caucasian therapist who spoke a foreign language to an Asian girl who spoke and thought in Cantonese. I could hardly be considered a valid competitor for those who gave her negative identity messages, probably in reaction to her acting out on her father and his new wife.

Yet if I could not reach into Fon's sense of trust and belief system, she would probably become a more serious self-injurer and develop other symptoms. I had to stress growth and not change; change would imply betrayal of what her parents had taught her. Growth would merely be adding to what she had been taught.

"So, English people put new words in your head. Did they erase the old Chinese words?"

She shrugged her shoulders. "No, maybe not."

"Maybe I'm going to put more English words in your head."

"What English words? Maybe not good English words."

I leaned forward. Our faces were two feet apart. I smiled sympathetically at her and answered her unasked question. "No, they will be good words. You need good words."

Her eyes became watery again. She blinked hard to keep back the tears.

"Bad girls must have bad words."

"I will decide if you are a bad girl or not."

"I know. *You* cannot decide."

Her voice rose. Her tentativeness was clear. The ice was cracking. It was presumptuous of me to suggest that I could usurp her preexisting thoughts and ideas.

Two days later, I walked to my desk and found an envelope on which was neatly printed: MR. LEVENKRON. I opened the letter.

> Dear Mr. Levenkron,
> I am like a bird with a broken wing. Mother bird throws broken bird out of next [sic]. No other birds want it. It is let to die. I don't like broken wing. Can you fix wing?
>
>   Sincerely,
>   Fon

I was surprised and relieved by the letter. Fon had apparently used her Chinese dictionary to talk to me. Instead of seeking supervision from a colleague for this unusual case, I signed up for a course in "Spoken Cantonese" at the China Institute in America, on Manhattan's East Side. I knew that I would need more credentials to gain her trust, to attempt to treat her.

I talked to Fon for the three years she was in the middle school. Her English improved at a far greater rate than my Cantonese. She always wrote to me in between talks. Her written English improved but her endearing Chinese idiomatic way of writing never changed. I always cherished her style.

She stopped hitting herself. She stopped referring to herself as a "bad girl," and went on to a high school for gifted girls. She never did make contact with her mother, who presumably remained in Hong Kong. In her last letter, she wrote about a boy she was seriously involved with and hoped that they would go to the same college.

Reaching In

What was the aspect of Fon's treatment that helped her transform her self-image as a bad person to one deserving of success and happiness? It was her ability to communicate her inner thoughts and feelings and have them validated by an interested person. By talking to me and finding that she could trust me with her worst thoughts, Fon was able to use her healthy attachment to me as a bridge away from her isolation.

Thirty years ago, beginning therapists were warned about the **Rescue Syndrome**. This was a caution that we not aggrandize our roles beyond helping patients clarify their problems. The modus operandi was that the patients must work, on their own, to change their behavior. To do more than this was to become directly involved in their lives, to become "real" people to them. An active role for the therapist was (and still is in some psychoanalytic circles) frowned upon because it might cause patient confusion and blend the therapist into the mix of their problems, "excusing" them from their own responsibility to create change within themselves.

Today's patients come to us with fewer support systems than ever: no extended family; broken, subdivided, blended, and reorganized nuclear families; sometimes repeatedly exhausted and depleted single parents. In addition, there is little or no sense of community, and less faith in religious institutions. It still remains the responsibility of the nuclear family to be the primary resource. If this is not available, today's psychotherapist is often drafted into the role of surrogate, therapeutic parent. This implies, if not outright rescuing, assisting, advising, then sometimes intervening on behalf of the patient, if she is a minor, with individuals and institutions. All of which is a far cry from the analytic couch of the last generation.

Self-mutilation also demands a team approach, including physicians and often psychopharmacologists who will evaluate, and prescribe medication where necessary. This means confidentiality is more defused among those who will be involved in helping the self-mutilator. It does not mean that the contents of the therapy session go beyond those clinically participating in treatment.

"Reaching in" implies such nontraditional concepts as intruding into the patient's ideas about herself, where they involve areas of erroneous negativity about appearance or intelligence, likability, and so on, and contradicting them. Such a move will be met with resistance, but behind the patient's resistance lies a wish that the intruding therapist is correct.

Treating the self-mutilator, in the beginning, often requires that the therapist adopt a highly authoritative, though warm, supportive posture. This will be regarded as trustworthy by the patient only if the therapist is truly comfortable with the features of such a posture. The therapist is appointing himself or herself as a guide for the patient who is lost.

The assumption here is that the therapist is familiar with the patient's character structure and has determined what developmental deficits must be developed (self-esteem, ability to communicate, etc.) in the therapy. A blind authoritarian approach is not recommended.

Reaching the Deflector

Meg, a fourteen-year-old girl, was discharged from a medical hospital after making a severe cut at her elbow joint, which severed the tendon and caused the loss of nearly a pint of blood despite her own efforts to stop the bleeding. Apparently she did not intend to wreak as much damage as she did. She called for her mother after her own efforts to stop the bleeding failed. She did not remember actually making the cut, but did remember the immediate aftermath.

As a result of the mother's and Meg's retelling of the episode to the hospital staff, Meg was not designated an attempted suicide but a self-mutilator. She was released from the hospital after three weeks in the psychiatric unit, on condition that she engage in intensive outpatient therapy.

Meg entered my consultation room and promptly sat down mechanically in the center of my three-seater couch. I greeted her with "Are you glad to be out of the hospital, or were you more comfortable there than at home?"

She shrugged very slightly. "The hospital was okay. It's okay at home," she responded in a monotone, her face expressionless. She sat straight, her hands clasped in her lap. She continued to stare straight ahead. I thought about all the questions I could ask her, envisioning all the equivocal, meaningless answers I would get. I decided to stop asking questions.

"If you hadn't cut your arm and were never allowed to hurt yourself again, you would experience bad feelings."

She restrained her emerging, startled look and remained silent for a minute.

"I don't know what you want me to say." Her tone was mildly plaintive.

"I want you to tell me about the bad feelings you have."

"I feel all right now."

"You don't always feel all right. When you don't, what *do* you think about?"

"I don't know."

"Your arm knows. It found out when you cut it." (I anthropomorphized her arm to create a metaphor for a dialogue between herself and her arm.) She was affecting a self-contained or isolated posture in order to remain hidden. I demonstrated that I knew she had strong negative feelings that were not only betrayed by her most recent cutting episode (she had thirty other cuts on her arms, thighs, and stomach, according to the medical examination). By characterizing it as an "attack" on her arm, I could characterize her as concealing aggressive feelings.

"Why did you say I attacked my arm?"

"If you cut my arm with a kitchen knife, I could say you attacked me, or you attacked my arm."

"But it was *my* arm. I can't attack myself."

"Cut me or cut yourself—it's an attack on one person's body or another."

"I don't get angry at anybody. I don't attack anybody."

"You attack yourself, so I know that you get angry at yourself."

"That's not the same. That's not real anger. Real anger has to include someone else."

"Who told you that?"

"Everybody knows that [reverting to a monotone]."

"Nobody believes that . . . but you."

She shifted in her seat, crossed her arms and legs.

"Anger is bad. I don't have anger."

"You aren't aware that you have anger. You don't want to be aware of that. Cutting yourself is like screaming out that you have painful feelings and angry feelings . . . everybody knows that."

Her face became more expressive. She looked confused, frightened. My complacency with such a powerful "accusation" unnerved her.

"Does that mean I'm a bad person?"

"It means that you are a confused person, who feels guilty toward other people and about your own feelings."

"Then I must be a bad person."

"No. You are not a bad person. You just can't understand complicated feelings, *your* complicated feelings. You need instructions so you can understand these complicated feelings. Then you won't have to attack your arm."

She looked at me meekly, almost pleadingly. "I wish you wouldn't say that I 'attacked' my arm."

"I will help you understand your complicated feelings. Then you won't have to damage or hurt any part of yourself."

"You think that my complicated feelings, as you put it, are connected to the cuts I made?"

"Yes, of course. It's clear that these cuts you make are powerful, dangerous, crippling, and bloody. These are hardly casual acts."

I could see the tension in her face as she reacted to the evenly stated but severe words about her actions.

Meg attended her sessions regularly, twice a week. She began to quote things that were said in sessions to her parents. They occasionally called me to tell me that she was becoming more enthusiastic about the things she was learning in therapy. She never cut herself again, and by the end of the first year of therapy, I went from doing ninety percent of the talking-teaching to barely being able to get a word in edgewise. Meg became a talkative, self-analyzing patient!

When working with many of my teenage patients, especially the self-mutilators, I find that initially I have to reach out to them and verbally draw them to me with statements about their unspoken pain, which is sometimes unconscious as well, and with explanations to their unasked questions. This, of course, involves some risks. When I begin with such a patient, in my own mind I'm digging in for the long haul . . . of talking, explaining, and teaching before expecting to be rewarded by responsiveness, trust, and attachment, the necessary requirements to fill the deficits that overcome self-mutilation, self-loathing, and low self-esteem. In order to do this, one has to keep in mind the following:

—Establish trust by letting the self-mutilator know she is understood.
—Allow time for trust to build a healthy attachment.
—Expect the self-mutilator to depend on that attachment during the course of therapy.
—Encourage the self-harmer to accept and incorporate the therapist's positive ideas to replace her negative self-image.
—Help the self-mutilator to build her own strength on the new positive ideas, thereby developing a healthy independence.

1 4

WHO CAN BE

THE HELPERS?

Since the chief characteristic of self-mutilating is physical wounding, a person who undertakes to help the self-wounder must have some knowledge of what constitutes physical danger and what does not. Talk about cuts and burns must not be overwhelming to that helper. If the self-mutilator senses fear on the helper's part, she will dismiss him or her as having no emotional value to her. The helper will have to be comfortable talking *casually* with the patient about the physical harm she does to herself.

Sometimes the context will be in asking about new injuries; other times the context will be looking at the wound, confronting (without drama) the infliction, interpreting the wound by its severity, and requesting the person to reflect on what her thoughts and feelings were preceding, during, and after the act. This process is important because it desensitizes the act of self-harming by removing the drama and replacing isolation with sharing.

Profile of the Effective Helper

If the self-mutilator sees signs of anxiety or nervousness on the part of a helper, that will make her disinterested and unreceptive to the offer of help from this person. Clearly, a helper needs certain personality traits in order to function properly:

- **Confidence**, which ranks very high on the list.
- The ability to stay **empathetic** and close to the patient when that patient hears her own talk as strange, even to herself; when her thoughts don't make sense; or acts she has committed against herself are mysterious to her.
- The ability to appear **knowledgeable** about her illness, her cutting, her depression, her low self-esteem, her feeling that she doesn't belong with others, anywhere.
- An **understanding** of her despair, and the ability to convey that understanding to her.
- A **nurturing** posture, continuously directed toward her, regardless of whether or not she requests it.
- **Optimism** about her future and ability to overcome the feelings that wear her down, such as wanting to give up, or to hurt herself.

The helper who combines all of these traits offers the self-mutilator a way out of her painful loneliness: their relationship. The patient will be suspicious and will test the helper repeatedly. While some of her testing will be verbal, for example, "I knew coming here, just sitting around and talking, wouldn't really help anything," some of it will be acts of cutting or other forms of self-injury. These must be attended by a physician, if they warrant it. So the helper has to be aligned with a physician who will accept the task of working with a patient who actively undermines her own safety, physical functioning, and health.

A parent should tell the physician about the self-mutilation and be sure that he or she is understanding, calm, and projects confidence. The physician, in this case, is continually cleaning up after her, knowing that she may "mess up" again, much as a mother changes a diaper knowing that the new one she has replaced the soiled one with will in its turn be soiled. Perhaps metaphorically, the treatment team is dealing with a person who suffers from unresolved infantile issues, such as a lack of basic trust.*

You may have noticed that this profile could describe a calm and confident parent. Working with a patient to repair childhood deficits includes a component of **reparenting**, which describes a psychological process of changing the parental stance to a warmly authoritative, more directive approach, making the self-harmer feel younger and more protected. In this state, she can accept support to build in the missing trust. But reparenting is not exclusively the province of the therapist. In fact, reparenting within these guidelines can be highly effective for parents; the child's first preference is to get what she needs emotionally from her own parents.

The Reparenting Relationship

At the beginning, the helper must do much of the talking. If he (or she) asks too many questions, the self-mutilator will infer that the helper is needy (of answers from her), and not knowledgeable. The helper is taking a gamble in making highly personal generalizations about someone he doesn't even know. But the patient won't really be looking to find an error; rather, she is hoping that the helper is right . . . most of the time. She does, deep down, beneath her despair, wish for a helper who can be depended upon.

*See Erik Erikson, *Childhood and Society*.

She knows that she can't help herself, no matter how much charm and bravado she exudes to others.

Occasionally, the helper will find himself bordering on the overconfident. It is better to make this error than to be so prudent and careful that he/she looks hesitant, and shaky. To illustrate this confident style, here is a typical exchange from a therapy session. As usual, I'm very active in providing answers rather than asking questions:

"You seem to have made quite a cut on your foot."

She shrugs, looking embarrassed.

"I'm going to tell you why you cut yourself."

She looks surprised and relieved.

"When no one can reach you, even though you can reach and affect others, you feel empty and unreal. Life feels unreal, hopeless, devoid of fun. You get unhappy, and after a while, depressed, flat, blah, no ups, no downs, everything starts to matter less and less. You begin to say to yourself, 'Why bother?' "

"How could you know that about me? I never told anyone about my feelings."

"That's not all I know about you," I continue. "I know that when you feel despairing and the 'why bother' takes over, that's when you are ready to cut or otherwise hurt yourself. At different times you may 'choose' to feel the pain or go into a trance, become numb and 'watch the cutting happen'—even though you're doing it, you feel like a spectator. It is at that moment that the 'why bother' goes away."

She shakes her head. "Everybody who comes in here asks me questions that I don't know the answers to. So I make them up. I make up some pretty good ones, too. But *you* come in here and you don't ask me questions, you give me answers to questions that I have about myself. I still don't know how you can do that."

She is gesturing wildly with her hands to emphasize her point. I smile at this emotionally lost thirteen-year-old.

"I guess there's a lot about yourself that you don't know. I think that you are going to need someone to help you learn those things, and help you grow up."

"Nobody can do that for someone else!"

"Oh yes they can. I can."

She looks worried. "But I'm the one who does that for other people. It would be too much for you to try to do that for me!"

"Apparently, you are too much for yourself to fix or help. But that doesn't make you too much for me. I don't even think that helping you will get me the least bit tired."

"I get everyone tired. And you'll get tired of me, too."

"I know you're not used to leaning on anyone. But I think that a small part of you is beginning to believe me—that maybe I have an answer to your secret wish."

Making a mock frown at me, "What secret wish?"

"The secret wish that someone *could* take care of you. That they would take such complete care of you that it would be as if you were a baby to them, and they would always be there to protect you and calm you down when you needed it."

Her eyes become watery but she flexes her face muscles to prevent the tears from falling. I lean toward her and gently tell her to let her face muscles relax. The tears begin to fall.

"I think that those tears mean you're beginning to trust me." I take a tissue and wipe her face. "I'm going to keep these tears in this tissue. They are precious tears; they mean that you can like yourself, and even hope for your future."

"Well, I don't know about that," she protests mildly.

"Well, *I* do."

Certainly, there are risks involved in getting so far ahead of the patient about herself. But these risks are less than they would seem, since the "knowledge" stated by the therapist is really quite general. Barring a unique trauma that began her illness, she would have had to experience such feelings. She desperately needs to know that she can be understood by someone who takes a parental posture toward her. She has already given up on the authority figures in her life.

These character traits and behaviors I have suggested for the therapist—warm and bossy, unflappably confident—must be real and comfortable to be effective. Parents can support the therapeutic process by adopting a similar style at home. If they have difficulty as they attempt a new style of interaction, they should consult a family counselor. The most successful treatment includes help and guidance for parents and other family members.

A Chain of Helpers

Often the therapist is called upon to loan some of the confidence described above to others who wish to help. The professional helpers include the psychotherapist, family counselor, physicians, and nurses involved with the patient. Nonprofessional helpers include a larger group: parents, grandparents, other primary caretakers, foster parents, siblings, close friends, and institutional helpers, guidance counselors, teachers, boarding school staff ranging from house parents to headmasters/headmistresses. At the college level, helpers include student services counselors, deans, and student self-help groups.

Those who would be helpers should expect differing levels of efficiency, different levels of success.

Looking for Behavioral Changes

In the area of behavioral change, which refers to eliminating self-harming behavior, placing someone in a psychiatric hospital produces nearly one hundred percent success immediately. The reason for this is that there is a staff of professionals observing the patient twenty-four hours a day, seven days a week, in an environment where nothing sharp is permitted and the windows are made out of plastic. Most conversations are with professionals who have therapeutic change as the goal of these conversations. Of course, hospitalization is temporary.

The outpatient therapist can be effective during the session, but the carryover after the patient leaves the therapy session depends on the level of communication and trust she establishes with those around her.

Family members who try to help a self-mutilator will experience much less efficiency in terms of how much their communication has improved the patient's frame of mind. There are several impediments to efficiency here. The first is their fear of causing an increase in frequency and severity of the dangerous behavior. The second stems from the first. Their fear leads to anger, which leads to guilt, which leads back to fear. For example, a mother notices a fresh cut, bandage, or bleeding. She questions the self-harmer, demanding an explanation. When none is given, she exclaims, "I wish you didn't have to do this to yourself! We're getting you help but you're still cutting yourself. Don't you see how crazy this is—I don't know what we're going to do with you."

The parent has expressed anger, frustration, and hopelessness—understandable but not helpful. Instead, he or she could make a statement demonstrating their understanding of the self-harmer's feelings: "I see you're having a bad time again. Do you want to talk about it with me? Maybe first we should go into the bathroom and put some disinfectant and a bandage on your arm." Here the parent has demonstrated empathy and also exercised restraint in keeping their own feelings in check so that they could bring a sense of calm to the situation. In this way, family members can be a valuable part of their child's recovery, but they must be supported by, and in communication with, mental health professionals.

Family counseling serves two purposes: first, it provides a con-

tinual flow of information and instructions; and second, it fur-
nishes emotional support since the child's "careful" behavior is
self-conscious and extremely draining of energy. As if this weren't
difficult enough for family member-helpers, they are still coping
with their own previous habits in relating to the troubled adolescent, which have to be revised. They usually are experiencing
feelings of guilt and blame as well. This gives the patient leverage
to use "angry cutting" as a weapon for release of built-up rage,
when it exists.

If family members have expectations that a change on the part
of parents or outpatient therapy will produce instant results, these
expectations need to be addressed. *Parents can become angry and frus-*
trated when they believe they have acted in helpful ways, have changed
much of their style of communication for the better, and their ungrateful
child still hasn't improved. In retaliation, they may revert to their former
postures and style of communication. They have, at that point, lost sight
of their child as a mentally ill person. But she is not in a reasonable state,
therefore, reasonable expectations are unreasonable.

Unless those who would help the self-mutilator are aware of
these tactical considerations, the helper can become the hopeless.
Expressions of helplessness or emotional demands placed on the
patient can impede progress. The process of recovery is in any
event lengthy and uneven. If the helper can maintain a hopeful and
calm presence, he or she will be making a great contribution.

When Privacy Becomes Isolation

Earlier, I stated that the profile of the effective helper could be described as that of a warm but bossy parent, unflappably calm in the
face of self-destructive behavior. A bossy but caring person is
sometimes intrusive when the occasion warrants—and self-
mutilation is just such an occasion. Privacy is highly valued in our
society and is usually a healthy part of one's life. But for the cut-

ter, who is an emotionally isolated person, privacy becomes a way of hiding. Therefore, intruding into the patient's privacy is an important part of treatment.

The first level of struggle with the illness is the effort to diminish and finally eliminate self-harming behavior. Cutting and burning oneself requires privacy, which serves several purposes:

- The absence of others means the absence of those who might interfere and stop her.
- Privacy means the absence of those who would distract her from going into a trance or from experiencing the anger that drives her to harm herself.
- Awareness of the presence of family members makes the cutter sensitive to the feelings of others who might react with anger, sadness, or fright. This would defeat the purpose of the behavior—to release unconscious pain in a manner not connected to others.

Though minimizing privacy is important, a therapist or family member cannot always be present when the act of self-mutilation is occurring. But examining the damage done, on a regular basis, creates the anticipation of nonprivacy or the expectation of discovery while the act is being committed. This makes the cutter less inclined to commit the act; emotionally, she is less isolated. Also she feels as if the self-inflicted pain is not going unnoticed. If someone she loves or depends on recognizes that she is hurting herself, this says something to her. It tells her that she is cared for and loved; that she isn't invisible.

The therapist needs specifically to question the patient as to whether or not there are newly inflicted injuries. If the answer is yes, or merely a shrug of the shoulders, the therapist asks to see the injury. This observation, when done consistently, creates the anticipatory sense of loss of privacy.

At the same time it induces a bonding on the part of the patient to the therapist, who by showing interest in and acceptance of the patient's "ugly [physical] side" will eventually be trusted to share the hidden emotional side.

Of course, the therapist has to maintain a level of talk consistent with this expectation. After all, the therapist is not a dermatologist whose interest is skin-deep. Since the therapist also is not a physician, damage to the skin whose seriousness is questionable should always be referred to a doctor. This will protect the patient from infection, excessive scarring, unrepaired tendons, and other consequences, as well as protecting the therapist from taking on more responsibility than he or she can handle.

If a therapist reacts to the damage by revealing their inability to treat the injury medically, this could lead them to show fear, anger, exasperation, and even to plead with the patient to discontinue such behavior. All of these reactions weaken the therapist's trustworthiness in the patient's eyes. The therapist should intervene by getting the patient prompt medical care, while dealing with the emotional issues.

In summary, *routine discussions of the injuries and deciding what to do about them increases trust, begins to integrate the personality's sense of relationship to another person, and replaces self-mutilation with attachment.*

Again, the personality of the therapist is critical here. The goal of this process is to have the self-mutilator relinquish her privacy and isolation for something more attractive—the connection to another person. This connection has to be safer, more secure, than the patient has experienced for a long time. The criterion of the security of the connection is how much self-harming behavior is exchanged for talk about feelings.

Of course, the real test of the therapeutic relationship is evaluated by how comfortably a patient can reveal, both verbally and visually, the results of her behavior. This presumes that her motives are not exhibitionistic, that she is not bragging or showing off. Ordinarily, self-mutilators are shy and ashamed about showing their handiwork to another person, especially someone who would know that the injury was self-inflicted, not accidental.

The process of unraveling the core of the disorder—that which holds it together and hides the real causes of unbearable feelings from the consciousness of the individual—increases the patient's discomfort. She has lost her "anesthetic" and has to cope with the emotional pain, the discomfort that her disorder has shielded her from. Now the relationship between patient and therapist is really tested. Will she go back to her former shield or tolerate the new discomfort in favor of the support, security, and trust that she receives from the new relationship? If she chooses to continue her recovery behavior, the relationship has passed a critical point and much more than her self-mutilating behavior will change.

Trust is being established, but the therapist helping her through this transition will have to expect some backsliding, both as an emotional testing by the patient and out of her fear of losing her safety shield. Unconsciously, the self-mutilator is afraid that the therapist will disappoint her and turn out to be untrustworthy. So she continues to test the strength of his resolve to help her.

The cutting may return after it has disappeared for a while, or it may take a turn for the more severe after it has diminished to minor scratches. Usually, it will not return to the kind of injuring that poses jeopardy and requires medical intervention. Through all of these changes the therapist, and hopefully the family, with professional support, can maintain a balanced, caring attitude. The self-harmer is more disappointed with herself than they may realize.

1 5

BUMPS ALONG THE ROAD

Psychotherapy is an opportunity for learning about healthy relationships: the relationship between therapist and patient teaches the self-harmer new ways of relating to herself and others. What is missing in the world of the self-mutilator is trust and healthy attachment to other people; these emotional building blocks can be developed within the therapeutic relationship.

Nurturant-authoritative therapy consists of therapist's behaviors that are caring, supportive, guiding, and instructive. These behaviors also include, when appropriate, both praising and warning. The patient receives the caring, turns it into trust, and then utilizes the trust to develop the confidence to try new ways of coping (suggested by the therapist). Confidence grows with each success: it reduces self-loathing, leads to increased bonding, raises self-esteem, and encourages verbal reflection, which finally replaces the self-destructive acts.★

★This therapy was first explained in my book *Treating and Overcoming Anorexia Nervosa* (New York: Scribner, 1982).

Nurturant-authoritative therapy has been developed to compensate for specific dysfunctions within family systems. These occur when parents become emotionally depleted and unwittingly communicate abandoning and *dependent* (needy) messages to their child. (In another form, parental neediness may include irritable, aggressive, and assaultive behavior.) The child believes that there is no emotional support available to her. She must invent a self-reliant support system, based on her own "successful" behaviors. The self-mutilator "succeeds" by tolerating pain; the anorexic by losing weight. The self-regulating behaviors replace support from others. Nurturant-authoritative therapy reverses this psychological process.

Often, though not always, the self-mutilator has a history of being hurt, harmed, or molested. When this is the case, *mistrust is her security.* She will constantly look for opportunities to mistrust her helpers. She often invites harming behavior from her helpers, thus confirming her need to mistrust them, as well as her need to hide and protect herself from those who seek to help her. She may do this in a passive manner by not talking during therapy sessions. Seeming to daydream in order to escape any connection with her therapist, she is in fact constantly testing. Her need to protect herself from others by mistrusting them could frustrate the less than determined helper.

The descriptions of therapy that have preceded this chapter have emphasized the positive, successful interchange between patient and therapist that has facilitated recovery. Now that a model for treatment has been illustrated, we must address what could go wrong. When therapy sessions or family interactions create a retreat to old symptoms, we need to understand why this has happened and how to get back on track again. There is rarely an instance of perfectly smooth treatment, or family change that produces a quick, steady recovery.

When treatment or family relationships seem to have retreated back to "square one," conferences are necessary between therapist and supervisor, or therapist and family. The self-mutilator may cling to old habits as far as trust goes but she really does want to change her familiar security-seeking patterns.

Mona: Two Steps Forward, One Step Back

Mona was referred to me at the age of twenty-eight. She was living alone, and abusing and harming herself in many ways. She had innumerable cuts, dozens on each limb, as well as on her stomach and chest. She had two burns, both from a teakettle full of boiling water, one on each thigh. She wore only crewneck or turtleneck sweaters, even in summer. Her father paid for all of her living expenses, which gave her extraordinary privacy to neglect and harm herself. She had drifted away from her friends, was unemployed, and could be uninhibited and irresponsible about her appearance. There was no one to ask her about "suspicious" damage that might show up rarely should a sleeve ride past her wrist, or a button on a high-neck cardigan sweater come undone.

Her previous therapist had just retired from analytic practice and referred Mona to me. She warned me that Mona could be a difficult patient and that treatment would proceed slowly, since she was granted a "fortress existence" by her father that supported her resistance to change. The analyst also diplomatically informed me that Mona could be "quite independent at times."

Mona entered the room with a pleasant smile, shook my hand, then became preoccupied with taking off her backpack, scarf, and coat. She placed them at the end of the couch, turned around to face me, and sat down. Her focus on the rituals involving in folding and placing her clothes and backpack, in blatant disregard of my presence, indicated her comfort with detachment from others. As she sat down, she resumed smiling, as if to say, "Now I have time for you." It was all very natural and devoid of hostility.

Part of the referral information received from her previous therapist indicated a history of physical (not sexual) abuse and of ne-

glect by her mother (divorced from her father for fifteen years
and now remarried). The abuse had begun when Mona was a
child and had continued through her young adulthood. Mona
never received a birthday card, or any other greeting card, from her
mother, even though she had sent her mother cards on Mother's
Day, Christmas, Easter, and her birthday without fail for the past
fifteen years.

At our initial session, Mona sat there with a friendly smile, saying nothing.

I was aware that her previous therapist was comfortable with si-
lences of up to ten minutes, so Mona didn't expect me to speak
for a while.

"I have been told by Dr. N. that you haven't had much experience with having your feelings of warmth reciprocated by those
closest and most important to you."

She brushed my comment off with a frown and a shake of the
head. "Whatever you grow up with, you think is normal. You just
take it as it comes."

For the first three weeks, Mona was pleasantly light in response
to questions about her discomfort and loneliness. She told me stories of punishment, assaults, and not being let into the house after
coming home from school on cold winter days. She seemed to regard me as sympathetic, which I had been, and easy for her to talk
to. We appeared to have gotten off to a good start.

Mona came in for her seventh session with a frown on her face.

"What's the matter?" I inquired.

"What's the difference?" she snapped back.

"You look upset. I'm concerned. Maybe if we talk about it, we
can improve the situation or how you feel."

Her face still maintained its hard look.

"You're concerned? You get paid. I think that you get paid for
squat!"

"Why are you angry? Nothing has changed. I've always been
paid. It never bothered you before."

"Well, maybe this just isn't good enough anymore."

"Are you saying that you don't want to continue therapy?"

"I'm saying that you're not able to do anything for me. Look!"

She lifted her long sleeve and pointed to a cut, three inches long, on the inside of her forearm. It was still bleeding through the gauze and tape she had covered it with. I walked over to my bookcase, took down a bottle of peroxide, adhesive tape, and gauze pads, walked back to Mona, sat down, and removed the bandage. I was surprised by the size of the cut. I poured the peroxide up and down—it erupted as a lake of pink foam. After a second and third application, the foam was white. I made a tight bandage to close the cut as much as I could. The gauze stayed white. The bleeding had stopped.

"You will have to go next door to my dermatologist colleague to see if it needs stitches or other treatment after our session is over. What is this about?"

I looked up from the cut to find a tearful Mona.

"Today's my birthday."

"No card?"

"No card."

"Do you understand why you were so angry at me when you came in today?"

She answered me in a tone that suggested I should have known the answer.

"You are the only person I speak to about my feelings. Should I have been angry with the grocer?"

"That's quite a cut," I remarked.

"There will always be cuts," she countered in a resigned tone.

We both stared at the white bandage. No bleeding observable. She rolled her sleeve down.

"Is that something you want to change?"

"The cuts? No, I want to be a mass of scars and bleeding my whole life, or until I accidentally kill myself."

I allowed for the sarcasm—anger takes a while to dissipate.

"So we have the same goals for you?" I offered.

"Some of the same goals," she grudgingly accepted.

Mona had come into her session angry, dissatisfied, acting as if she wanted to end the relationship. She did not have the relationship skills or the ability to reflect upon what was really bothering her. At the age of twenty-eight, she was doing what an early adolescent does: she yells at her mother or father for a grievance that belongs somewhere else. Ironically, Mona was snapping at me over a grievance she had with her own mother. Another birthday passing without hearing from her mother had been a painful reminder of her mother's neglect.

Therapy offered Mona a new opportunity to learn that she could depend on another person. By dressing her wound, I did what a parent would do. This would deepen her trust and attachment to me and would provide me with more leverage to help Mona.

My goal was to develop her verbal expressiveness, which would in turn give her more insight into her own feelings, especially her anger and sadness. I knew from her symptoms she had no healthy outlet for emotional pain. I would continually push her to clarify the reason behind every self-harming act until the act itself became unnecessary.

Therapy: A Relationship Laboratory

Here again we see that much of the psychotherapeutic approach in treating self-mutilators is a kind of reparenting. This includes directing the patient, arguing with the patient, even apologizing to the patient. The therapy becomes a laboratory where the patient can experiment with new interpersonal behaviors and experience their outcomes in relative safety. This explains why therapists proceed with great care and planning as to their own behavior and responses. The nurturant-authoritative relationship is more real than most therapies allow for; it contains more risks of the patient acting out and in rare instances even terminating treatment. I say rare instances because most patients, like Mona, are looking for a person who will give them fair, caring guidance. On some level, these patients know that they need to acquire facets of personality development they are missing.

Life has taught the self-harmer not to trust anyone, or in less severe cases, to be extremely wary. She will set up many tests for a person to pass before taking even a limited chance to risk such trust.

If she interprets a person as suddenly *un*deserving of trust, she withdraws it and retreats. That does not mean that treatment and trust are not able to be restored. Parents have the same worry: If they say the wrong thing to their disturbed child, they will lose the child's love forever. Neither is true. Behind the tough mask lies the need for trust and dependency. In other words, whether we are parents or therapists, they are rooting for us. Even when a patient pulls away in fear or anger, we can redeem their trust.

In the case of Mona, she would skip several sessions in a row, return for a half-dozen, and then fade out again for one or two meetings. I didn't make an issue of her erratic attendance since she was an abused child who now was at an independent age, and would probably flee anyone who was critical of her. Her erratic attendance did persist for the entire first year of treatment; by skipping appointments, Mona was showing me how hard it was for her to accept care from another person.

In her second year of treatment she skipped less than one session in five, and her cutting occurred only twice, and they were minor cuts. But she remained erratic in her attitude toward therapy and questioned whether I could help her improve the quality of her life and feelings about herself. She could be withdrawn during a session, yet by the end of the first year she would attribute her mood to a situation beyond therapy rather than act it out on me.

Our relationship became more complex. Mona would ask for my advice, support, and guidance about issues that ranged from interviewing for a job to taking a trip with a family member or friend.

She did relinquish her housebound lifestyle and took two jobs so that she could achieve financial independence from her father. She gave up all self-harming behaviors, started on an antidepressant (which we first discussed for six months), contacted friends she hadn't spoken to in years, and could by then be termed symptom-free.

Hazards on the Road to Recovery

We can expect certain situations and events to cause unevenness in recovery; they threaten treatment by destabilizing the patient's perception of the therapist, or of therapy, and in turn demoralize the therapist with regard to his or her effectiveness. These situations include the family's resentment of the time recovery takes; the amount of money it costs; and the inconvenience that traveling to see the therapist imposes on the family. And in more than a few cases, jealousy on the part of one parent of the therapist's confidential relationship with his or her daughter can threaten or even end therapy.

Adverse statements to the patient by family members may make her feel guilty and withdraw from therapy. When the therapist notices poor attendance, or a continuing flatness in the patient's voice demonstrating disinterest no matter what is being discussed, it is a good idea to question the patient about how the other members of her family see her being in therapy.

What follows is a case where a family secret created a roadblock to recovery.

Ainsley: Hiding the Harm

Ainsley was a precocious-looking fourteen-year-old who from the first session struck a pleasantly disengaged posture in answering all questions with either "I don't know," a shrug of the shoulders, or "I don't know what you want me to say." Her parents would not meet with me in the same room at the same time. They were uncommunicative with each other at home and seemed on the verge of separation. I referred them to a marital therapist, insisting that they do this to help their daughter. They agreed to begin weekly couple sessions.

Ainsley had made several severe cuts on her upper arms and the upper part of her breast. Two of these episodes landed her in a hospital. She had been transferred to psychiatric units where she proved uncommunicative, though pleasant. Psychiatric tests were ordered and they indicated that Ainsley "would not project"—in other words, she didn't respond to the pictures presented to her. The technical conclusion was: "Unusual degree of constriction in thought and speech indicating depression with the possibility of childhood trauma which she cannot consciously cope with," which indicated to me that Ainsley would have a very hard time expressing herself, or even thinking about her problems.

The psych report was accurate. She couldn't seem to use our sessions to talk about anything that bothered her. Yet she came in without protest. Ainsley continued to attend sessions for a while without disclosing anything of consequence or for that matter initiating discussion about any subject or event in her life. Her facial expressions seemed in conflict with each other. On the one hand, she seemed to want to please me. On the other, she seemed to be prohibited from answering my questions.

Then the therapist who was working with her parents called me one day to tell me that Ainsley's mother had made a comment during their session that he thought bore repeating to me. Her mother had said that she thought her daughter liked me, and went on to say that "he would be the kind of personality to tempt my daughter to cooperate with therapy."

He thought her characterization of me as a *tempting* personality suggested the possibility of incest behavior somewhere in the family, though he couldn't speculate who the parties involved were.

This information enabled me to rethink the behavior of this mysterious patient who seemed satisfied with our sessions even though they were devoid of any meaningful content. She liked the benign tone that existed between us, but did not dare embark on a path of communication that could eventually lead to disclosures that were forbidden. Disclosures that might cause family disruption and acrimony, that might damage parents. Even the beginning of disclosing communication, no matter how innocent the subject might be, might weaken Ainsley's guardedness and allow for further drifting toward importantly secretive areas.

Finally, I decided to confront her.

"You seem to respond to me with great care," I began.

She looked puzzled and a little alarmed. Could she have disclosed something? "What do you mean?"

"I have listened to your responses and interpreted them as behavior, instead of just focusing on the words that you were saying."

Now she looked more worried (and more expressive) than she had ever looked in session before.

"You seem to react to my questions as if you don't understand them or the answer to them could be yes or no. By saying this you are saying that the question doesn't really matter, since the answer doesn't matter."

No response. Despite her obvious discomfort, I continued.

"It's clear that you don't permit yourself to say *anything* here that would really matter. That would be dangerous and therefore prohibited."

"I don't know what you want me to say."

"You have often said that before, and I have usually responded by telling you that I had nothing special in mind and I was merely offering you a chance to talk about your thoughts and feelings. That's over now. I'll *tell* you what I want you to say."

She looked frightened, but I had to help her let go of the secret that I suspected was destroying her.

"I want you to tell me if there are family secrets about physical and possibly sexual contact, or even sexual talk, at home? That's a 'yes' or 'no' question because I am asking you if you have heard, heard about secondhand, or seen or experienced these acts I have just mentioned."

I made strong eye contact with her so she could not slip away from the demand and intensity of the moment.

"I don't know," she replied shakily.

"This is a yes/no question. If you don't answer no, then the answer is not no."

She looked increasingly agitated. "Well, I *don't* know . . . there might be."

"Between whom?"

She looked down at the floor. "Not between anybody and me."

"Between which person and which child?"

"Between my mother and my brother. And my mother and little sister, too. She's eight years old."

Her jaw was set. She looked angry.

"Are you angry about it? You look angry right now."

"I guess so. I think that it's wrong to do."

"Who is doing what to whom?"

Ainsley looked straight at me. "I have never seen or heard anything happen, but my little brother complained to me a couple of times that he thought he was too old to be bathed by our mother at the age of twelve. He especially doesn't like that she cleans his— you know—private parts."

"Do you think that this is unnecessary, or improper?"

"I think it's weird, maybe sick. I don't think it's good for my brother. If my father wanted to bathe me, I would run away from home, so I must think it's pretty bad that she bathes him. What if my family is crazy? Will my mother go to jail because I told you?

When she knew that my brother told me, because I asked her about it, she told me never to tell anyone about it or the family would fall apart. She told me never to trust anybody with any information about the family because it might lead to me telling about this. She was right, but I think I'm glad I did. I couldn't talk about anything at all before."

"To answer your first question, no, your mother won't go to jail for bathing your brother, but she will have to answer to people about her behavior and your brother will be interviewed. If nothing else has occurred, your mother will be warned not to do this or anything like it again. She will either be mad at both you and your brother, or glad that she was finally stopped from doing what she knew was wrong. It's too soon to say which."

"Do you have to tell her that I said it?"

"Not directly. We'll make sure it comes out. We will talk to your brother before we talk to your mother so what has been happening becomes a family disclosure, not someone telling on your mother."

Ainsley looked relieved. "Maybe we can talk about real things now."

"You're entitled to," I responded.

Ainsley delved into issues I had previously thought she wouldn't. We discussed her precocious dress and manner. Her mother had led her to believe that children were supposed to evoke sexual ideas in their parents. In effect, Ainsley had adopted this seductive style in reaction to her mother's behavior with her brother and sister, as well as the instructions regarding secrecy. Her mother's behavior and conspiratorial manner are hallmarks of the incest victim, and indeed that was the case with this parent. After discussing this, Ainsley stopped dressing seductively and flirting in the style of an older teen.

She talked about cutting herself out of frustration with her mother's behavior toward her siblings and her own feeling of being trapped with too many secrets. There was no way to get information from others about all her confusion. She always felt the pain when she cut herself. Sometimes if no one was around she would shout or grunt as if she were attacking somebody else.

———

The course of Ainsley's individual therapy demonstrates the struggle between symptoms (her cutting) and attachment (a therapeutic relationship with another person) and so will be discussed further in the next chapter.

As to family treatment, social workers interviewed her brother, and couple's sessions were held with Ainsley's parents in which Ainsley's mother discussed the abuse she had received at the hands of her own father. Ainsley's sister was seen by a child psychiatrist. The couple did become divorced and the father retained custody of the children.

Ainsley gave up her cutting and continued therapy for three years after that session. She remained in regular contact with her mother, though her brother had little to do with her until he was sixteen. He had not gotten over his anger toward her and went into therapy himself. Their father remarried and her mother became involved with an incest survivor's group.

A number of factors can sabotage treatment and recovery, but often they are hidden from the view of the therapist. The therapist rarely has the opportunity to acquire information that the patient is keeping secret whether out of loyalty or fear. It is even more difficult when the unknown information is outside the patient's awareness or consciousness. If patient and therapist are lucky, all the information necessary for treatment will finally emerge and help to promote recovery.

16

CAUGHT BETWEEN

SYMPTOM AND ATTACHMENT

W hen the barriers to trust between helper and helped are finally brought down and the self-mutilating behavior is nearly extinguished, the patient experiences relief as well as a sense of loss at the surrender of her symptoms. Relief comes through the newfound sense of trust that she has developed for her therapist, and others around her. Her new sense of trust, healthy dependency, and attachment become evident when she walks into her therapist's office and begins with, "You'll be so proud of me when you hear how I handled this situation with my friend—you know, the one who always gets her way and takes advantage of me."

The ability to assert her needs may be an ordinary experience for a person who has always had many close relationships in which she feels accepted; but to the self-mutilator, this is a new experience.

At the same time she is experiencing pride and rising self-esteem over her new assertiveness, she is in conflict. She is still in mourning over the loss of her cutting behavior, which she has turned to for relief from emotional distress in the past. She may feel as if she has lost her most reliable friend.

The therapist must continually help the patient to maintain her attachment to him (or her) and never take it for granted. The patient, after all, still is in constant conflict between her desire for human attachment, trust, and intimacy on the one hand, and the isolation and mistrust that gave rise to her illness on the other. In many ways, she has been more comfortable in the role of being isolated and distrusting than that of being intimate, and she is still vulnerable with her new feelings about herself.

Mona (chapter 14) persisted in coming to therapy with cuts she had made the day before her session. They were still open and sometimes still bleeding through the bandage. There were two interpretations I could make about her behavior: the first was that she wanted me to see what she was doing to herself so that I could continue to take her seriously, which would reassure her that my own efforts on her behalf would not slacken; the second was that she wasn't yet sure she could give up her safety behavior for the nearly abstract idea of interpersonal trust. Clearly she was in transition, caught between two emotional methods of survival.

One of the ways I could encourage the interpersonal choice to prevail was to intrude upon her cutting defense. I would notice if there were any new cuts, and if there were, I asked to see them. This might involve taking off a bandage or just a Band-Aid, but it is an experience that exposes the privacy of the defense of cutting by allowing another to see it, to make interpretations or judgments about it, or to scrutinize it.

This revealing of a once-secret defense devalues it. It should be done at the beginning of each session until the cutting stops. If the cutter is aware that a cut will be examined after each episode, she will begin to imagine that the therapist is attending the episode at the time of its occurrence and analyzing the reason for doing it.

Eventually the anticipated analysis of the reason for it replaces the act of cutting.

When painful issues in the life of the cutter develop, she is more likely to resort to cutting and become angry at the therapist for her painful feelings and his failure to prevent them from happening or not banishing them immediately. This immature thinking on the part of the patient will mature as the therapy progresses. It is important for both the therapist and the family to have patience with the initial immaturity of the cutter's expectations, as well as the rate at which she matures during the course of the therapy.

If we keep in mind that this kind of a disorder develops out of deficits in coping with painful feelings—whether they are caused by trauma, hereditary chemistry, family problems, or social, school, and educational problems, among others—then we are aware that building defenses to replace deficits and the symptoms that have filled in for them takes time.

If showing the therapist the self-inflicted injury is one kind of message, a more serious message to the therapist comes when appointments are canceled for insufficient reason, or simply failed when the patient doesn't call and doesn't show up. This usually means the patient is choosing her old mode of self-harming and is hiding from her therapist, who represents attachment.

When Mona didn't show up for one appointment, I called her apartment, only to get her answering machine. I left the following message: "Mona, we had an appointment today at four. Please call me to explain why you didn't come without notifying me so that I will know that you are all right. I confess that I am suspicious that for some reason you avoided me today, so let's clear this up as soon as possible."

After a while it feels as if there are three of us involved: the two facets of Mona, her healthy wish to be well and her disorder, and myself. In some sense the three of us argue while in session. Mona becomes the rope in a tug-of-war between her old posture (self-mutilation) and her new one of attachment encouraged by me.

For my part, I do my usual examination of the newest wound and occasionally point to or refer to all the older scars to remind her that this accumulation of scar tissue hasn't produced anything lasting for her, just a batch of "quick fixes." She acknowledges this and shrugs her shoulders.

"It seemed like the only thing to do at the time," she responds.

"That time is over. This is a new time and you know there are alternatives," I might mildly admonish her.

At this point, the style of our dialogue has changed. It becomes implicit in our relationship that I hold her responsible for her self-harming behavior. That doesn't mean that I don't expect her to do it any more, but there are rules or understandings that we have about cutting. She must tell me when she does it. She must show me the injury. We must then discuss why she did it. If she violates this understanding, then she is answerable to something like a scolding. Our agreement doesn't demand total abstinence but it does demand total disclosure.

When this point is reached in therapy, then the patient is much closer to the "attachment" end of the continuum than to the isolated, self-mutilating end of it. It's not the cure, but it's progress.

Ainsley: Making Progress

With Ainsley, our difficulty was making initial movement toward meaningful contact as a prerequisite to attachment. Ainsley had instructions from her mother not to form a therapeutic connection with me and I was unaware of that until an outside person (her parents' therapist) suggested the possibility to me.

Ainsley and I had interminable sessions where nothing important was said and I had my doubts about the outcome of this therapy.

When the major goals of therapy consist of changing the way the person relates to those around her in terms of trust, attachment, and dependency, versus the way she uses harming her own body to compensate for her inability to do so, unblocking the barriers caused by existing relationships is just as important as any insights she needs to develop about her own mental makeup.

As you recall, once the incest secret was out, I made it clear to Ainsley that my goal was not to make her like her mother less, or to take her place. She slowly became freer to talk. I also explained to her that nothing she said in the privacy of our meetings could possibly hurt her mother. She was leery of this but gave it thought and gradually began to discuss each member of the family with me.

We started with siblings—not looking for faults, just general descriptions of their personalities and the way each relates to other members of the family. We progressed to parents much in the same manner. We spent many months in the second year of therapy dealing with material about the family. She had a difficult time because in the privacy of the office she was making a critical statement about a member of her family.

"It gives me the creeps. I don't really know how to talk about this. It's not that I'm jealous of them. I feel so ashamed that there was something sick going on. I hate this—I feel bad even discussing it with you. My mother has always told me never to trust anyone outside the family or tell them anything about us."

"Well, you're going against her instructions. Are you sorry?"

"I'm nervous but not sorry. I still don't know what to do about what happened between them."

"What is your worst fantasy about their secret?"

She looked startled. "I could never say it . . . to anyone."

"If you could never say it to anyone, because it's so terrible and unspeakable, then you must feel somewhat alone in your house?"

She whispered, "I guess so."

"And?"

"Angry and guilty." She looked indignant. "After all the consideration I give everyone in that house, I shouldn't have to contend with this."

"It sounds like you feel that they're being insubordinate or disobedient toward you."

"I guess that's not right?"

"It's not that it's right or wrong, but it does interest me. You can feel angry, jealous, left out, or worried. Any daughter or sister in your position would feel that. But the last part is more in the province of the head of the family, a parent. Do you feel like you're a parent in your family?"

Shrugging, "Sometimes, I guess."

"Parents get angry at their children. Do you get angry at other members of your family?"

"I get angry at myself."

"Nobody else?"

"Never."

"Do you punish yourself?"

"Yes."

"Does that solve anything?"

"Temporarily. It solves whatever's the issue at hand."

"You were referred to me because of a secret you were keeping from everyone, cutting yourself. That *is* how you punish yourself, isn't it?"

"Yes. I guess so."

"Perhaps before we attempt to unravel anyone else's secrets in the family, you and I need to uncover your secrets, within the confidentiality of our sessions."

"How will that help?"

"When you punish yourself, you don't really redress any of your grievances with another person. It doesn't change any of their behavior toward you or even cause them to offer you an apology. When you confront them, something real happens between two people, not just between you and your skin."

I was devaluing Ainsley's solution of cutting herself and substituting her cutting with communication. After that session, she chose to violate her mother's admonition. Ainsley discussed her father's temper; memories of her mother's going into trances and not remembering ordinary events of the day; and strange, conspiratorial glances exchanged between her mother and her sister. It was clear that Ainsley felt she had grown up in a house of strangers. If she adopted the role of nurturer, she would feel less dispensable in the family. In this way she had learned to repress, or ignore, her own emotional needs.

The entire family required extensive treatment to deal with this and other damaging issues, which did result (as we saw) in her parents getting divorced. Her sister started to talk about visual and auditory hallucinations she was experiencing. She was put on medication in addition to intensive individual therapy.

The family code of silence nearly prevented any therapy from being effective in bringing all of this to light. Ainsley had to choose between the risk of entrusting another person with her secret ideas, and her feelings over the cutting that she was using as a safety valve which allowed the family system to go on in its dysfunctional, destructive manner.

Cultural Clashes

Usually, a person elects to participate in psychotherapy. But there are exceptions: people who are either suicidal or pose a danger to others may be remanded by criminal or family courts to undergo psychotherapy or face various threats, involving custody of their children or even imprisonment. There are also people who have disorders that don't fall into these categories but *not* to seek treatment is regarded as dangerous. Minors and their families may find themselves seeking psychotherapy for psychological problems, such as anorexia nervosa and self-mutilation, even when the very idea of psychotherapy is culturally or religiously repugnant to them.

Parents may fear that psychotherapy will alienate their children from the family's religious roots. The immigrant family may feel that their cultural values will be compromised if their child trusts someone outside their own culture. It is important, whenever possible, for the therapist to address these fears with the parents of a minor before beginning individual therapy if there is the possibility that these concerns will polarize the family against the therapy. In such cases, the therapist is facing a quasi-voluntary patient or patients. A family that has these fears will look for a quick end to symptoms. They may remove their child from therapy prematurely, inviting a return of the original symptoms or other symptoms.

Tula, eighteen years old, came to the United States from Eastern Europe. Not unlike Fon (in chapter 13), Tula had difficulty with her English, living in Astoria, New York, where one can get along without speaking English except in school. She was referred to me by a pediatrician practicing in Astoria who was concerned about various cuts he had seen on her arms and thighs. At first he considered calling Child Welfare to investigate the possibility of child abuse, but given his position in the community and his evaluation that these were self-inflicted wounds, he decided to call me. I agreed to see her.

Tula sat on the couch in absolute stillness as she told her story. She was pale and thin, and her voice was barely audible.

Tula's father was a religious man, who held his minister in great esteem. When his daughter, a recent high school graduate, was offered a job as assistant to the minister in a neighboring community, she took the position.

The minister was a likable man, always bringing her little gifts, boxes of chocolates and desserts. After a month, he began to make sexual overtures to her. Soon they went from subtle—his hand on her thigh—to more intrusive and invasive. He told her it was part of God's plan and it would serve her well later in life as preparation for marriage.

Tula's conflicts grew greater. She was sure that she was doing something wrong, but there was no one she dared ask. Like a trapped incest victim, she had nowhere to turn. She couldn't go to her parents and make them choose to believe her and attack a reputable holy man.

She began to vent her anger at being exploited by cutting herself. She started the cutting high up on her thighs, partly as a rage against her sexual organs for attracting the minister's attention and desire, but also with the unconscious hope that the cuts and scars near her vagina would repel him and cause him to lose interest in her. When that failed, she made cuts on her breasts, partly because of the pain it created, venting anger on this part of her body that attracted him, and again also hoping that he would find her unattractive because of these cuts and scars. He only laughed cruelly and offered to add to her cuts.

None of Tula's behavior discouraged the minister from his sexual aggressiveness. When he raped her, she made a huge cut down the top of her thigh six inches long, which landed her in the emergency room of the local hospital. It was at that point that she told the admitting psychiatrist her story.

She was not a minor and requested that he not tell her parents. He did get her permission to call her pediatrician. In conference they decided that they could recommend psychotherapy as a requirement to keep her information confidential, and Tula readily agreed.

When she returned home from the emergency room, she told her parents that she had accidentally cut herself out of frustration from working for the minister. She described him as demanding, impatient, inappreciative, and grouchy. She told them that she hated working for him. They were surprised at their daughter's reaction to a well-regarded man of their church, but responded by instructing her to get a paying job. (The church position was voluntary.)

When Tula told them that the doctor strongly recommended psychotherapy, her parents objected. They felt equally strongly that psychotherapy might replace church teaching and European traditions. Her parents were mystified and threatened: first Tula leaves her job within the church, and now a recommendation of "outside" help. But Tula insisted, telling them that she had done things like that before to herself, and that the doctor said she might accidentally kill herself if she didn't go into therapy.

She felt both guilty about disagreeing with her family and relieved that they reluctantly gave their permission without finding out what really happened between herself and the minister. Her guilt would make it difficult to disclose her thoughts and emotions in therapy, since she felt that by talking to a therapist she was betraying her parents.

"This psychotherapy is not the way of our people. We turn to each other, or to God and His church." Those were her father's parting words to her when he dropped her off at my office and drove away.

Tula was frightened during the first four interviews. I understood that she probably feared the same behavior from me that she got from the minister. Her fear, coupled with her father's disapproval, provided ample reason for her to prove unlikely to benefit from individual psychotherapy.

During the second month of sessions, Tula began to be forthcoming about the details of the minister's behavior toward her. She spoke slowly, explaining, "I'm always afraid that you will think that I'm a liar and a bad girl. I never even had a date with a boy or a man before I met the minister or since. I don't think that I ever will again."

She was a modest girl, as befitted her European upbringing, and when talking about the incidents remained as vague as she could while making sure she was communicating what had happened. It was understandable that it would be difficult for her to impart

CUTTING

this kind of information. It was her feelings that she had the most difficulty in expressing.

I said, "While you have explained that you are concerned with my opinion of you for the information you are giving me, I am wondering what you are feeling as you are telling me these things, or how this whole experience has affected you?"

She looked puzzled. "What do you mean?"

"While you have given me concrete descriptions about what has happened, I am left wondering what the girl in the story feels like because of this difficult experience."

"I cannot talk about my feelings. They are private. I don't talk to my parents about them. I cannot talk to you about what I have not already talked to my parents about."

I was treading on dangerous ground. Tula saw me as asking her to be disloyal to her family by talking personally about herself to an outsider. Not only was I an outsider to her family but to her community. It would be some time before she would talk about the cutting she was doing. It would be a longer time before she would stop cutting, since a prerequisite to ending the cutting involved both sharing her acts and the feelings connected to them, and then cooperatively analyzing the reason for these acts and understanding how grievances can be redressed on an interpersonal level.

This process took about three years. It involved her family getting used to her talking to me, as well as their stating to her that it was all right to disclose whatever was necessary for her recovery. In addition, I had to help her develop a language in which to talk about these complex feelings. This language did not exist in her family's vocabulary. Ultimately, she did acquire competence in self-reflection, and in interpreting her feelings and thoughts.

This issue of cultural or familiar loyalty should not be confused with resistance due to psychological blocking or conflict. It is actually a healthy, socially learned restraint to communication and indiscreet familiarity. It becomes obsolete in psychotherapy, however, and even hampers recovery, since a willingness to develop a rapport with the therapist is the first step in developing an attachment that can be used for therapeutic change.

Clearing Away the Barriers to Attachment

Very often the patient who seems unwilling to talk is hampered by barriers such as those discussed above: family secrets; family instructions not to trust anyone outside the family; family instructions not to trust anyone from a different ethnic, religious, or cultural group; and loyalty, defined by using the family to solve all emotional problems.

When a patient appears constrained, prevented by some invisible prohibition from either talking freely or responding with more than a "Yes," "No," or "I don't know," the therapist needs to ask the kinds of questions that will expose barriers to therapy.

Some of the many possible questions address these issues directly:

"How does your family feel about your being in therapy?"

"Is either of your parents embarrassed, ashamed, jealous, worried, or guilty about your coming here?"

"Are issues of cost, or insurance reimbursement, ever brought up by your parents?"

"Do you feel guilty because you've come to see me?"

"Have you been told not to tell anyone that you are coming here?"

"Has anyone else in your family ever been in therapy?"

"Do you worry about what others will think about what you might say here?"

"Do you worry about others finding out about what you say here, either because of a breach in confidentiality, or because you might slip up and report what you've said?"

Obviously, many more questions can be used to break the stalemate of lack of communication. Once that stalemate is broken, a dialogue will begin to develop that is the beginning of the attachment–trust–dependency relationship. This leads to the patient's incorporating the therapist's value system, one that proves that communication within a significant relationship makes self-mutilation unnecessary.

1 7

MOVING BACKWARDS

TO RECOVERY

What course should treatment take once the behavioral symptom of self-mutilation has stopped? Is the patient cured? We have examined the growth of self-mutilation from **feature** to **disorder** and described this process. As a full-blown disorder, it poses cosmetic, medical, and life-threatening dangers. The treatment process that leads to recovery is not a shortcut from disorder to health, but rather a shortened reversal of the first process.

Medicine, when faced with an inoperable brain tumor, tries to utilize nonsurgical techniques to shrink the tumor until, hopefully, it is operable. Psychology and psychiatry must shrink the disorder, self-mutilation, back to the feature it was when it began. When the patient has decreased the use of this symptom for the relief of anger, hopelessness, terror (in the case of incest), or despair, then other preexisting problems will reemerge.

Usually, self-mutilation is the last in a chain of symptoms to develop—probably because short of violent suicide, it is the strongest experience of all symptomatic behaviors from the standpoint of pain, and of visually witnessing one's own blood.

If this is the case, self-mutilation is at the top of the pyramid of psychological problems that an individual may suffer from, the tip of the iceberg. Underlying it reside all the disorders and problems that it hides. As psychotherapy shrinks this "psychological tumor," instead of healthy tissue, or mental health, being uncovered, we enter the areas of hidden problems it had formerly masked.

One of the most common of these problems is anorexia nervosa, or bulimia, referred to as "the eating disorders." As someone reduces or eliminates cutting, in the case of the anorexic, she then begins to lose weight. In the case of the bulimic, she increases or resumes her binging and vomiting. It must seem to many therapists and families that the reward for success in one area is a demand to tackle many other problems and crises.

One of the major arguments posed against behaviorist treatments of many psychological disorders is that they invite the next level of the mental illness pyramid to emerge. Without an in-depth understanding of the disorder on the patient's part, not only will another symptom come along to replace it, but the originally identified disorder is likely to return repeatedly as well.

Successful treatment requires that *all behavioral change be accomplished within a trusting treatment alliance,* meaning a trusting therapeutic relationship, otherwise the change is superficial, fragile, and usually temporary.

For the patient, psychotherapy is no less than an undertaking to change one's mental and emotional personality organization. As if that isn't a big enough commitment, add to this the feeling that the person who makes the commitment doesn't know what changes are waiting for him or her around the next corner.

Melanie: A Dissociated Self-Mutilator

Melanie, nineteen years old, had been hospitalized in three separate psychiatric hospitals and had been in outpatient individual psychotherapy for three years. She had been diagnosed originally with anorexia nervosa, then with bulimia, then for cocaine and alcohol abuse, and lastly with an unclear diagnosis lying between suicidality and self-mutilation. Due to the severity of some of this mutilation, it was difficult for the psychiatrist to decide whether the cuts represented frank suicide attempts or were deliberately self-inflicted for reasons discussed in previous chapters.

Her answers to questions at the admitting interviews at the hospitals amounted to: "I don't know if I wanted to kill myself. I can hardly remember how I felt or even what I did to myself." These answers are typical of the **dissociated** self-mutilator, the more disturbed of the two categories.

As treatment progressed in therapy with Melanie, she was able to express more of her revulsion at the pronounced an ugly-looking scars that covered her arms and shoulders. She resolved never to cut herself again and in fact her cutting diminished rapidly. In the first six months of treatment with her, I recall two incidents of minor cutting and then none in the following year.

As her cutting diminished, however, I noticed that she was becoming thinner. When I asked her about her eating and weight, she replied that she had allowed herself to gain too much weight and that she hated being in her body, or looking in the mirror at this weight and appearance. She was five foot five inches tall and weighed one hundred and seventeen pounds. When I asked her what her goal weight was, she said that she intended to reduce to one hundred pounds.

These urgent feelings about her need for weight reduction were not expressed while she was cutting. Though she could not make a cause-and-effect connection between giving up cutting and experiencing an intensification of her anorexia (and bulimia), the timing of the shift in Melanie's symptoms was more than coincidental.

During this same period of time that she started losing weight, she began occasionally to use cocaine and would call me in a state of severe inebriation to jokingly suggest suicide.

Using medications to lessen her anxiety and mental disorganization was a tricky process. Since her past history consisted of mixing alcohol and street drugs with her medication, a physician dispensed her medication in three-day doses to avoid overdosing and "mixing." This wasn't a guarantee, since Melanie had been known to hoard her medication until she had enough to put herself at risk if she resorted to combining it with alcohol.

The two modes of treatment for such a difficult patient were hospitalization, or inpatient living, which at some point became financially unfeasible; or frequent outpatient visits (three times a week) to maintain a "competitive attachment" to therapy, versus symptomatic behavior. The latter was chosen, as she had used up all her hospitalization insurance. Medication was administered as described above.

The next stage of recovery for Melanie was her giving up cocaine and alcohol, which was accomplished over the following year, during which she entered college on a part-time basis.

The last stage of recovery, which will be the longest, will involve giving up her obsession with eating and weight and the concomitant disordered behavior: limiting her calorie intake, abusing laxatives, and vomiting, along with dangerously strenuous exercising.

––––––––––

If the treatment alliance is not carefully maintained through each stage, ideally with the same therapist, recovery can quickly reverse itself right up the ladder of relinquished behaviors. When this happens, therapy must be intensified to stop the relapsing.

When a patient suffers a setback and a symptom that was improving worsens, or more seriously when a relinquished symptom returns, both the therapist and the patient's family can become very discouraged. They need to remember that recovery is uneven and such setbacks are not necessarily an indication that the treatment is failing. Each setback has to be analyzed in terms of external events—what has gone wrong? Identifying the various stress factors has the effect of calming the patient, the therapist, and the family.

Confidentiality and Behavioral Disorders

When a person has been exposed to a cutter, she enjoys very little confidentiality so far as her symptoms are concerned. Often scars or bleeding are spotted by members of the family; sometimes hospital emergency rooms are involved to repair damage done to the skin, nerves, and tendons.

If a patient has sought therapy for mild anxiety or depression, the progress he or she is making is subtle, as is the unevenness of that progress—subtle enough to elude the observations of others, even family and friends, on a short-term basis.

The cutter, the anorexic, and other behaviorally disordered individuals, however, cannot conceal the success, stagnation, or worsening of their problem. It is apparent to all those close to them. In addition, both the therapist and the family experience more worry when they don't perceive steady progress, and can be thrown into desperation, even panic, if they see a relapse. This is due in part to the dangers associated with behavioral disorders and the sense of urgency to complete recovery. Everyone involved wants assurance that the symptom is gone, never to rear its frightening head again.

Because the symptom is so clearly observable, two important confidentialities are jeopardized: the patient's and the therapist's. I am not suggesting that therapists are not accountable for their success or failure, but the extra pressure of the family's sense of urgency can hamper progress. In order to preserve patient confidentiality *and* to reassure the family, the therapist should let the parents know that they will be informed if there are any dangerous setbacks or injuries.

Dual Diagnosis

If the patient has more than one disorder that has been diagnosed, we classify this person as presenting a **dual diagnosis**. This term characterizes the patients discussed above—for instance, a person who self-mutilates and also has an eating disorder or drug abuse problem. These people are the most difficult to treat and pose the most dangers to themselves. In addition, they have the least even rate of progress toward recovery, the most conspicuous combination of symptoms, and therefore the least confidentiality. They also need the greatest number of specialists—often two for each disorder:

- The cutter requires a psychotherapist, a psychopharmacologist for prescribing medication, a physician to make medically necessary repairs, and occasionally a surgeon if the damage needs it.
- The anorexic requires a psychotherapist, often a psychopharmacologist, an endocrinologist, a gynecologist, and a nutritionist.

If drug addiction and alcoholism are involved, add to the above lists a detoxification unit, and specialized group meetings for members with the same problems.

It is less common, but not rare, to encounter a dual diagnosis patient with all of the symptoms mentioned requiring all these specialists and services, if the likelihood of recovery is to be maximized.

This can prove overwhelming for the parent to orchestrate, especially if the patient becomes reluctant to cooperate. Ideally, the psychotherapist should coordinate the various helpers as well as convincing the patient of their importance.

I entitled this chapter "Moving Backwards to Recovery" to

emphasize that cutting is not just a bad habit at the optimistic end, or total, hopeless mental illness at the pessimistic end. It is a highly complex collection of mental defenses, which manifest themselves through behaviorally self-destructive physical acts but conceal a host of emotional problems and developmental deficits.

Holly: The Dual Diagnosis Cutter

Holly came for treatment at fourteen years of age. She was well-groomed and unusually articulate. Her parents were both academic research psychologists at prestigious universities. She was just at the end of that awkward stage of puberty—braces on her teeth, legs too long for the rest of her body, feet and hands too large for her limbs, and with a gangly way of walking and gesturing.

She was referred to me for two problems, cutting and anorexia nervosa. She had recently been released from a psychiatric hospital with the warning that if she lost five pounds, she would be rehospitalized. When I weighed her, I realized that she had been pushing the limits assigned to her. She was five foot two and weighed ninety-two pounds. Her hospital discharge weight was ninety-six.

Holly's physician, while doing a routine physical examination, took a stethoscope to her chest only to find parallel cuts three inches long across her newly developing breasts. He did not make the assumption that this was a suicide attempt, though he reflexively shifted his eyes to her wrists, where he saw no cuts. Instead, he matter-of-factly asked her, "How come the cuts?"

Holly, who often used playfulness for deflection from confrontation, responded, "Mostly boredom, I guess. I don't think they'll scar. I bet they go away, not like tattoos—they're permanent."

The physician, keeping his cool, responded with, "Oh, we should be grateful that they're not tattoos now?"

She shrugged. "Could be worse."

The time for playfulness was over. "You're charming and likable, Holly," he admonished her, "but those red lines are a road map to severe trouble. Thanks for the smiles, but we have to refer you to someone who will change the direction you're secretly heading."

She offered no resistance. "Okay."

"Do you want to talk to me about it?"

"Nah, too long a story. You don't really have the time and I don't want to ruin a good day for both of us."

"You're a good caretaker, Holly. Maybe too good. I'll have to tell your mother about these," he said, pointing to her chest.

She looked at him, alarmed. "Do you really have to? I'll catch hell at home."

Two weeks later, she came into my office with the same cheeriness she used to fend off the world from identifying her unhappiness.

"Hi. I'm Holly and Dr. Gilbert says that you're a good therapist."

Holly presented a seamless picture of the well-adjusted early adolescent. There was nothing in her likable demeanor to suggest the turmoil beneath this facade. She looked more like the finished product of a successful course of therapy. As her therapy began and continued she would look less mentally healthy. This was to be a trip backward, from the shiny facade to the well-disguised pain.

I addressed her opening comment. "I'm sure that Dr. Gilbert wants good care for you."

She slumped a little in her chair as the realization sank in that she was already identified as a person in need, an identity she concealed to the best of her ability.

"I have a few problems that bother everybody else."

"Are you saying that your problems don't bother you?"

"Not quite. I'm saying that I wish they didn't bother everyone else so much. I think that I can keep them to myself and take care of myself."

I pointed to the stack of hospital reports on the desk. "It seems that whether you like it or not, others, professionals who might have a clearer perspective on your problems than you do, including a pediatrician who has known you since you were born, disagree with you."

She shrugged, a bit more timid this time.

"So why don't you, instead of all the others," I gestured to the stack of papers on my desk, "tell me who you really are and what hurts you so badly that you have had to resort to cutting and anorexia?"

"I guess Dr. Gilbert is right. You sound better than the last two shrinks and I've only been here a few minutes."

"I can see that you're funny, very smart, and psych-lingo savvy. But all these traits haven't helped you. Your symptoms keep screaming, 'Help!' "

"My parents are both psychologists. That doesn't help."

"No, they're not. When it comes to you, they're parents. I'm the only therapist in the picture."

"So, what are you going to do for me that they can't?"

"Find you."

"You might not like what you find."

"I will probably like what I find and have a tough time convincing you to like and accept who you are."

She stared at me unflinchingly, making intense eye contact. It looked like skepticism, but I kept going.

"Beware of me. You'll have a tough time coping with me because I won't let you hide in here. You can't be alone when you are in the same room with me."

"But I'm good at being alone."

"Are you starving when you're alone?"

"I'm also good at starving."

"I'm sure you are. I see tears of starvation in your eyes."

"What other choice do I have?"

"I'm going to invite you to depend on me."

"What if I'm too difficult? Will you quit?"

"What do *you* think?"

She looked at the floor, watching her tears fall. "I hope not, and I hate to hope."

"I am inviting you to hope. It will be okay."

"Nobody ever said that to me before."

Holly came to therapy three times a week for the first two months, eager to fill me in on her complaints about her parents' empty marriage, their mutual but separate professional conferences and research projects. Her complaint was that they both ordered her around and yet seemed intimidated by her at the same time. She complied with their demands for fear of wounding them.

Her posture toward me and the therapy sessions began to change. Her eagerness, positive attitude, and talkativeness gave way to increasing withdrawal, and "yes" or "no" answers to open-ended questions.

Her cutting had ceased. Her pediatrician verified that in his two examinations spanning six weeks there were no new detectable scars, lacerations, or burns. But she had lost that fifth pound. This gave her no leeway to avoid rehospitalization should she lose any more.

I had asked Holly about her cutting and weight without mentioning her weigh-ins or the hospital possibility. She answered sardonically that I shouldn't worry, she had both areas under control. This kind of withdrawal was not unusual for a patient who had surrendered so many long-term symptoms for a comparatively new relationship. She was not feeling relief from her underlying feelings of insecurity, of not belonging, of having no one to depend upon emotionally at home. At home she was simultaneously contemptuous of both her parents and compliant toward most of their wishes so as not to overpower them, at least in her own mind.

In withdrawing from me, Holly was doing what she did with

her parents. She had no experience with being a trusting, dependent child, so she would move away from anyone who couldn't make her feel secure enough for her feelings of distress to diminish. In the case of her parents, the insecurity was caused by their obvious unhappiness and their inability to rise above their own emotional exhaustion and depletion in order to offer her reassurance, warmth, and comfort when she required it.

In the case of her relationship with me, her insecurity stemmed from the limitations of the timed session, the scheduled visits to my office, her awareness that I had other patients, and that I was paid a fee to meet with her.

Adolescents who are neediest for attachment experience the most suspicion that the therapist will be more interested in another patient; many even pretend to themselves that they are the therapist's only patient. Their fantasy is that the therapist's sole motive in seeing them is his or her caring for them, and they block out the issues of illness and recovery that brought them together to begin with.

Just as older symptoms often return in the "progress" of therapy, the therapeutic relationship goes through a critical period of reversal as the patient sees her fantasies of being quickly and totally rescued from her own negative feelings (and sometimes from her parent's) evaporating. She begins to detach from the therapist and the process of therapy. She cancels appointments, comes late, leaves early, resorts to extensive periods of nonresponsiveness, and may discourage the therapist just as her returning symptoms discourage her family.

Are We Going Back to Square One?

It is at this point that a member of the family usually calls to find out why their daughter seems to be getting worse instead of better. When this occurs, it is a good idea for everyone to get together for a family meeting. Holly had shown me one side of her personality for the first two months. Now she was beginning to let her more angry side be seen by me. The family therapy session posed a sudden threat to Holly since her parents would be in the same room with me and she had been posturing differently to us. She would not know which posture to take, or which Holly to be. She was not yet ready to reveal the full extent of the sneers and other forms of rage that she directed at her parents, even though she was beginning to offer me samples of them.

Holly and her parents were expressionless in the waiting room when I went out to greet them. As they entered my office, their *family faces* emerged. The father was attempting a smile; the mother looked mildly annoyed at her husband, but when she turned in Holly's direction, she looked sad and intimidated. Holly looked like the proverbial ice queen. Her jaw was set, her eyes narrowed, her lips tight against each other. Her head was turned at a forty-five-degree angle toward her mother. It was quite clear who her expression was aimed at.

"I see lots of different moods in the room," I began.

Holly's father responded affably, slowly, in a philosophical style, "Well, we're a complicated family filled with complicated people."

It was difficult to tell whether he was finished talking or was being interrupted when his wife commented, "Oh, all the other families seen here are simpletons?"

Holly looked in my direction and rolled her eyes in response to her mother's comment, or to their interchange. "We are also a family in which each member is from another planet," she said sarcastically.

Both parents turned toward their daughter, whose chair was between them. They looked embarrassed. Holly had been afraid that her other self would be revealed to me, but in reaction to the setting she decided to ally with me and embarrass her parents.

I looked at Holly's father and addressed his description of the family. "It seems that you are an angry family suffering from a lot of disengagement from each other." He nodded in agreement. Holly's mother looked sad and Holly began to cry. I had never seen her cry before.

Then she said: "If I wasn't born, there would be no family. You two never would have married, or you'd be divorced by now. If I'm the reason that you're staying together, *please* accept my permission to get divorced. Look!"—holding up her arms—"I don't even cut myself anymore. If that was keeping you together, it's over. Yes, I know that I have other problems, and I'm not making any promises about them going away, but I hate living in our family."

Her father, trying to be the voice of reason amid the turmoil in the room, intervened. "Holly, honey, what kind of change would make you *want* to live in our family? We *are* capable of change, if that would help you."

"I don't think that the two of you are capable of the kind of change necessary. I don't think that you two love each other anymore, but I think that you're both doing an excellent job of being civilized about it. We don't have fighting in our family, we rarely disagree; as a matter of fact we—correction—the two of you hardly talk to each other at all. You don't have to be a psychologist to pick up on that." Holly reached for a handful of tissues.

At the end of the session, Holly's mother assured her that they would work on their relationship with a marriage counselor and attempt to improve it as much as possible, or consider divorce, but things would not continue the way they were. Each of them gave Holly a hug and a kiss separately as they left.

In the sessions following the family meeting, Holly resumed a positive attitude toward her therapy. She had adjusted her expectations of therapy and our relationship to a more realistic perspective.

She remarked during the first session after the family meeting, "First it looked like our relationship was going backwards. Then it looked like my progress was going backwards, and it still might, a little more, but I'm trying. Now it looks like my parents are going backwards. What's next?"

"I don't know, but I guess we'll keep digging until we hit bottom and there's nowhere to go but up."

"I hope we can hit bottom fast so we can start going up."

When a patient presents with cutting as a feature of her entire collection of psychological disorders, it is less deceptive both for the family and for the therapist to understand clearly how complex the treatment(s) will be, and how lengthy the amount of time that this will take.

If the self-mutilating has reached the status of disorder, it conceals the other problems that lie beneath it—from the patient herself and from those around her. Over time, as the self-mutilating symptom diminishes and the other psychological symptoms appear, it may feel to the family that there is no end of sickness possible. As a result, they may become discouraged.

A therapist familiar with the patterns this disorder can take will need to anticipate the emergence of other problems and communicate them to the family—ideally, before they show themselves. This minimizes discouragement on both the patient's and the family's part, as well as pressures on the therapist's optimism and morale. It also avoids a split between the therapist and the family that would hamper recovery, especially in cases where many specialists are involved in treatment.

It is essential to maintain a unity among all the helpers in the face of this daunting illness.

1 8

ACHIEVING GENUINE
COMMUNICATION
WITH OTHERS

Assertiveness Testing

As recovery progresses, the patient has learned how to translate her feelings into words, rather than act out these feelings in self-harming behaviors. She has learned to utilize help from another person to do so, and now has the emotional leverage of this relationship with which to test out her new verbal thinking and talking skills, with others, outside the protective setting of therapy or any other caring relationship with which she has accomplished these achievements.

Her therapist or other helper must now encourage her to express her likes and dislikes to others, both within her family and in social settings. The results of this stage of treatment are reviewed in meetings with the helper or therapist.

Typically, such a patient has a history of not being able to confront others, or even to disagree with others over such routine matters as which movie to see or which restaurant to eat at. She has usually been more comfortable as a secret dissident follower, unhappily acting as if she agreed with other people's choices. Throughout, she has remained compliant, obedient, passive, and falsely cheerful about decisions that include her and demands made upon her. She has learned not to care about her own needs, or to develop opinions and choices about minor as well as major issues that affect her.

Her "assignment" therefore becomes developing **assertiveness**, whether it is to initiate a plan with friends or family, or to disagree with a plan initiated by another if it displeases her, i.e., defend her personal rights. She has been most comfortable in the role of one who nurtures, supports, and agrees with others. A more assertive role at first will make her uncomfortable and anxious, fearing that she will be disliked if she is seen as demanding.

This issue has to be discussed at length and weekly reports of appropriate shifts in her behavior toward others should be reviewed. She is not asked to become a troublemaker or manufacture false issues with which to disagree, only to protest decisions that are truly to her disliking.

Coaching and Role-Playing

A therapist or other helper can coach her as to how to handle an anticipated conflict. **Role-playing** becomes very useful here. In this exercise, therapist and patient have practice discussions, often exchanging roles, to prepare for possible confrontations. Let's see how this is in fact done.

Elaine: Role-Playing in Action

Elaine, who had given up both her anorexia, prior to entering college, and her cutting, during the first month of her freshman year, was still unable to be assertive. She joined a sorority. It quickly became apparent to the other girls that she didn't drink alcohol and that she was not on "intimate" terms with boys yet. She was liked by the other girls but teased as the "virgin goody-goody." Elaine needed to prepare a response to her sorority sisters, one that could express her real thoughts and feelings without alienating them.

In sessions, we discussed her lack of readiness for romance and her unwillingness to drink alcohol. She could feign drinking by pouring herself club soda with a twist of lemon, so she wouldn't be teased, or try the alternative—demand that the other girls simply accept that she doesn't drink. She preferred the latter, so we role-played her statement of her choice, with myself playing the part of her friend.

"Elaine, what's the big deal about having one drink and loosening up a little? It might even help you be more relaxed about guys."

"I don't need to be high to enjoy myself. I don't need any artificial 'loosening up,' as you put it, to enjoy a guy. I can do that all by myself, without the help of alcohol."

"But you are never with a guy except your guy friends. How come?"

"Because there isn't a guy I met yet that I want to be more than friends with. Maybe I'm just fussier than everyone else. I'm not saying that's better than anyone else, or worse, for that matter, it's just who I am. Can you deal with me being that kind of person?"

I felt that this last demand would stop the other person from harassing her on those two issues, so I called an end to the role-playing.

"Elaine, that was very good. It only took us three times for you to get to that level of assertiveness. Do you think that you could say that in the sorority house if you're teased about those issues again?"

"I don't know. I was a little surprised at what came out of my mouth just then."

"Was it sincere?"

"Yes."

"Then why not try telling others who you really are?"

"What if I get them mad at me?"

"What is the worst scenario you imagine about them getting mad at you? They already tease you. Do they dislike you?"

"No. I think that they like me okay."

"Then you think that this kind of conversation would make them change the way they feel about you?"

"Probably not. It's just not me . . . to be disagreeable."

"Would you rather the teasing went on until all the boys involved with the sorority joined the girls and you became 'defined' by that phrase you complained about before?"

"So there is no easy way out?"

"I think that when you're changing your style and posture with others it has to make you tense, but that's better than putting up with what was happening before."

"You think I'll lose progress if I don't change?"

"What do you believe?"

"I think I'll want to hurt myself—because I'll get so mad at them."

"What you're saying is that if you don't get assertive with them, and stop them from treating you like you're inferior and not grown-up enough, you'll get inwardly angry at them and take it out on yourself. And that can't possibly change their behavior toward you or redress your grievance in any realistic way."

"I guess I hardly ever think that I can change anybody's behavior toward me."

"I guess it's time you gave it a try. Oh, and don't worry. They can't hear your heart pounding from nervousness."

Elaine had her confrontation, much along the lines we practiced, and it produced the results she hoped it would. The girls backed down on their teasing and her self-esteem rose.

Elaine could now attend socials at school without fear of being called the "virgin goody-goody." After a while most of the talk behind her back dropped off.

Elaine felt a sense of victory and was pleased to see that boys who came to the sorority mixers approached her, not having been warned off her by gossip. Within a year of this change, and a few light dates, Elaine became involved with a boy who was as shy and inexperienced as she was. This involvement raised her status among the other girls in the sorority and everyone stopped noticing that she didn't drink alcohol. Her own self-confidence was growing.

One day she came into my office looking serious. "I have to ask you something important." I nodded and waited.

"You know how many scars I have. What do I tell Bill about them? How much do I tell him about my problems? I haven't even told him that I'm in therapy. Should I tell him?"

"What is your greatest fear about telling him about the scars, past problems, and that you are in therapy?"

"That he'll think I'm crazy, mistrust me, or even break up with me."

"I imagine that he's already familiar enough with you physically to have seen many of your scars, is that accurate?"

She blushed a bit and nodded.

"Has he ever asked you about them?"

"No, he's not the pushy type. I mean, we exchange information about each other, but we know to wait for it to be offered. Neither of us asks for what hasn't been brought up by the other. We're both equally private and shy, I guess."

"Do you know if he's ever been in therapy?"

"No."

"What would you think if he told you that he is, or has been in therapy, and has had problems in the past, and still has unresolved problems that he's working on?"

"I guess I would wonder what they were and would want to know about them."

"Why would you want to know about them?"

"I guess I would want to know that he wasn't a killer, or a pedophile or anything perverted like that."

"Do you think that your problems fall into the category that you just mentioned?"

"No, I guess not. But I am ashamed that I did those things to myself."

"Do you think that you're attractive?"

"I guess I'm okay but nothing great."

"Do you think that Bill thinks that you're attractive?"

"He's always saying that he thinks I'm gorgeous. I think he's crazy, but I like hearing it."

"Do you think that you are a harsher judge of yourself than Bill is?"

She nodded in resigned agreement. "So I *should* tell him?"

"It's a big secret to keep. I think it will be hard for you to feel secure with him if you feel that he's in love with a false personality you have created. I don't recommend that you tell someone about this on your first date, but if you're seeing each other for months and maybe getting serious about your future together, it might be time to get ready to tell him."

"But what if he leaves me?"

"I don't believe that he will leave you, but I can see you're worried."

"Do other girls feel like this? You know, ashamed of themselves? Scared about new people in their lives finding out about the cutting?"

"Your fears are understandable, Elaine. But don't lose sight of what you know—Bill cares about you. And in many ways, we all have scars."

Elaine decided that we would discuss this in future sessions, until she felt ready to tell Bill.

Echoes from the Past

Elaine's questions and feelings are representative of those expressed by many people who have been through therapy. Though they consider themselves recovered, they still feel frustration and regret that they ever had the problem to begin with. They also feel sad about the lost years when they might have enjoyed their adolescence, or their young adulthood, or some other segment of their lives.

The last part of therapy should address these issues, especially with people who have had what I term **behavioral disorders**, which were obvious to others and at the same time crippling to their development. During her illness, those around the self-mutilator wanted to shout at her, "Are you crazy? Why don't you just stop hurting yourself?" The recovered cutter forgets what she was going through at that time and now asks herself the same questions: "Why was I so crazy for all those years? Why didn't I just stop it?"

Those who remember the turmoil remain sympathetic to the person that they used to be, and have less regret to deal with. Forgetting may buy one kind of peace but produces other problems, just as being currently unaware of emotional pain can produce mental illness.

Elaine had achieved a good level of recovery and was using her therapy and role-playing to prepare for real-life relationships. Other self-harmers need a longer time to recover, and their milestones of recovery are marked by an increase in communication, first with the therapist, then with others. We see this with Sonia, whom we first met in chapter 3.

Sonia: Communicating with the More Troubled Patient

Though some self-mutilators recover, do not resort to their old self-destructive behavior again for long periods of time (several years might serve as a criterion), and are not tempted to cut or burn themselves, others find the behavior persistent. Even with effective treatment, they could be described as chronically **recovering** as opposed to **recovered**. This is not to suggest that the patient will never achieve recovery. That will vary from individual to individual. But the behavior and temptation to do it again will persist for an indefinite period of time.

Sonia, the cellist, had experienced so much neglect and verbal, emotional, and physical abuse throughout her formative years and after that complete recovery for her would be years in coming, if ever.

One day she came into session looking very unhappy. It had been four months since she had cut herself; she was beginning to think of herself as recovered, finally. She hadn't carried anything with which to cut herself for a year and had only scratched herself once in the previous eight months. That was the incident four months earlier. We had both discussed it as being one of the mildest, in terms of damage to herself, that she had ever done. It was a bump in an otherwise nicely progressing recovery.

Today, she looked sullen, weary, hopeless. Silently, she shook her head. She sat down, continuing to shake her head, staring at the floor. It was clear that I would have to break the silence.

"Sonia, you are showing me with many gestures that something is seriously wrong. Now I would like you to *tell* me what that is."

Sonia's style had always been to express herself with gestures first and words last. Postponing talking as long as possible, she pulled up her left sleeve to show me the underside of her forearm, which had a two-inch diagonal cut, clearly made with some sort of blade. The cut was crossed at three points with adhesive tape strips that ran almost completely around her arm for maximum anchoring. She had fashioned three butterfly clamps to reseal the slit that the sharp instrument had made in her skin.

I remained silent as I looked closely at the cut.

"I'm never going to get better. . . ." Her voice trailed off. "I really believed that I was finished with it. Now it's back. The cut is deep. It's long. There was a lot of bleeding at first, until I sealed it as hard as I could. I even put an icepack on to stop the bleeding as soon as possible. I almost used a tourniquet, but it was too awkward, so I held my arm above my head, taped, with an icepack on it. I wanted it undone, not to have happened, to go back in time!"

I didn't steer her away from her bad feelings too quickly. That would have made her angrier at herself and angry at me for making light of it.

Matching her seriousness, I responded with, "This is the most serious damage you've done to yourself in a year."

"So, you see. I'll never get better. After all the new *insights* I've developed, the new *coping mechanisms* I've substituted for cutting, the new *language* I've learned to express my feelings [all said in mocking sarcasm], here we are!" she shouted, waving her injured arm at me.

"You are as angry at me as you are at yourself. You are feeling that both of us have failed. If I had not failed you with that list of 'growth items' you just named, this would have never occurred."

She looked alarmed. I was the closest person she had ever expressed anger at directly. And this was the first time.

"No, you misunderstand me! It's not *your* fault! It's me. I'm hopeless. You have good methods. It's just that nothing will work with me."

Sonia was frightened to see me as less powerful and all-knowing than she had come to expect of me. Our relationship had parent-child elements to it and no child wants to see her parent devalued. Then she would be alone, parentless. Sonia had to make it exclusively her fault if she were to be able to keep me intact as a dependable person. She yelled at me as a child blames a parent when she is angry at herself.

I had to help her reestablish the value of her therapeutic progress in her own mind.

"Is the way you reacted emotionally after cutting yourself, and the actions you took immediately afterward to treat the wound, the same as you would have done three years ago—before we began treatment?"

"No," she responded grudgingly. "I would have watched the blood run down my arm, even stain my clothes. I would have wanted to take a bath in my blood. I would have cleaned it up and concealed it afterward to avoid getting caught."

"Were you in immediate danger of getting caught this time? Is that why you took such quick and effective steps to end the episode?"

"No. Nobody else was home. My mother would not be home for hours."

"So why the rush? You could have let yourself do some more bleeding before repairing it."

"Because I don't *feel the same way about it* anymore. I hate it now!"

"Could we call *that* progress?"

Relief swept across her face. The devaluation she had conferred on us both was receding.

"So does that mean I'm not hopeless?"

"It means that your recovery is slow and uneven, which is frustrating to you, but *not* hopeless."

"So when is this going to be over?"

"You want the date?" I smiled. Sonia returned the smile.

"Yeah," she replied, nodding for emphasis.

————————

Sonia's scenario demonstrates a slower rate of progress than Elaine's. Many issues affect these differences in progress. Elaine was not abused by her family. Though there was some parental friction, it could not be considered severe. The presenting symptoms of these two girls contrasted strongly in the area of communication, and the degree of acting-out behaviors. There may even be genetic or chemical differences in their respective predispositions toward anxiety, panic, and depression. That, of course, is purely speculative since we have no way of measuring this factor.

There is also a contrast in the emotional health of these two girls' parents, as illustrated by the differing behaviors directed toward each by her parents: Sonia's parents were abusive and Elaine's were not. I am not suggesting that Elaine and Sonia are at opposite ends of the spectrum. There are cutters healthier than Elaine and sicker than Sonia.

Sonia had made remarkable progress in her communicating skills with me (sarcastically alluded to above), but had a great deal of difficulty in confronting others and verbalizing her dissatisfaction with their behavior or choices. Her wishes had been so violently denied and crushed in childhood that the risk of expressive communication with others outside the therapy office terrified her. This last cut was in reaction to a boy who came an hour late for their date, took her to a movie she didn't want to see but was afraid to object to, and wanted to return to his apartment with her to "fool around" sexually, with which she also passively complied.

We spent the next few months role-playing situations where she would have to say, "No," or, "I'd rather do something else," or, "What I'd really like to do is . . ."

Whereas Elaine could risk a new "script" with others, Sonia, due to her past history, needed much more reassurance and practice, to state her wishes or objections to others.

Our meetings involved role-playing similar to the work I did with Elaine, but I had to begin by playing both roles at once. For example:

"John asks you to go to a bar with him for a drink. You answer, 'No, I'm underage and I don't have a phony I.D.'

"He assures you that they are casual at this club and won't check.

"You reply, 'I don't like to drink anyway. It makes me uncomfortable.' "

Sonia looked worried as soon as I explained the script. Reflecting her worried look back to her, I asked, "Is there anything in this script that doesn't represent your true feelings?"

She shook her head as if all speaking was suddenly dangerous.

"Sonia, say, 'I'm underage and I don't have a phony I.D.' "

She stared at me for a minute.

I went on, "We are not up to the part where you object yet. We are building up to that with an excuse to see if he takes the hint."

That seemed to make it easier.

Slowly, almost inaudibly, she began, " 'I'm underage and I don't have a phony I.D.' "

"Sonia, that was good. Now try it again louder."

Eventually she would get so used to repeating the answer that she would be more comfortable with its confrontational nature.

After a month of rehearsing various statements of objection, and choices, Sonia walked into the office one day with a big smile on her face.

I responded with "Yes?" in anticipation of good news.

"You're going to be so proud of me! Wait until you hear this! He did ask me to go to a bar and I said all the stuff we went over, and he backed down because I said it *made me uncomfortable.* I didn't think that my feelings or wishes were reason enough for anyone to change their mind about anything!"

"Do you think it will be easier for you to tell people what you want or don't want to do in the future?"

She chuckled and rubbed her hands together. "Yeah, you bet. This is only the beginning. I know I won't always be able to do it, but I bet I do most of the time."

"I think that you'll discover that once you believe that you can express your needs and get them met, you'll take more chances in getting closer to people. You will have faith in yourself that you can protect yourself from others, should the need arise."

Sonia seemed transformed from the shy, frightened victim I met three years ago to someone who was anticipating a bright future. She still understood, however, that her recovery would be a bit bumpy and that she would experience some of her old feelings, especially in times of stress.

The issue of whether or not someone will never repeat her symptomatic behavior again in her life is simplistic. We all learn to express our hurt through certain actions and reactions very early on in life. If life is good to us, we will never have to reexperience old feelings and reactions that we have outgrown. If life presents us with extreme disappointments, tragedies, catastrophes, on the other hand, then we may react to previously outgrown actions *temporarily* until the situation has passed. We do not go back to square one. We have a setback and then it passes.

Sonia began to make rapid progress in improving her social life with both girls and boys her own age. As new conflicts arose, usually about minor issues, Sonia would come in and announce the conflict, then she would request a role-play with me to "solve the problem." When the "script" succeeded, she would come in the next time all aglow: "I did it! It worked!"

Eventually these requests diminished and we reviewed situations she could approach without a script.

For many individuals whose social development was impaired by their withdrawal into mental illness, therapy must not only help them to become healthier within themselves, but must teach them how to cope better outside the therapeutic environment. Whether they have been in a hospital, a residential treatment center, or an outpatient therapist's office, their recovery must include coping better with the rest of the world.

1 9

ANALYZING AND

CONFRONTING THE PAST

Although it is not fashionable to blame others for one's problems, certain problems are unmistakably linked to the awkwardness, ignorance, indifference, insensitivity, and yes, even malevolence of a family member and others in close proximity to the victim. The milder adjectives at the beginning of this list require less intense confrontations between family members.

Where serious confrontations are necessary, often it is better to have them take place in a therapist's or family counselor's office. This type of family session is especially important when destructive acts, such as physical abuse, have to be dealt with.

Incest and Physical Abuse

Confronting the person who inflicted the original physical or sexual abuse allows the victim to stop hurting herself. Remember, the victim thinks that she deserved the abuse, or that the abuse was normal and therefore should either be continued by others (battering husbands) or self-inflicted.

In confronting the abuser, the victim reinforces what she has learned in therapy: *that adults are responsible for their actions toward children and that there is no excuse for blaming the victim of abuse.* It is important to focus her anger on the perpetrator, pending an apology, so that she can heal from all past experiences. This will enable her to give up subsequent disorders that were developed in order to adjust to the original damage, as well as to repeated attacks.

When confrontation is not possible—whether because of a lack of willingness on the part of the perpetrator, geographic unavailability, the extreme age or death of the person (or persons) involved—the recovery is far more difficult to achieve. These confrontations are extremely difficult for all parties involved; it is important to understand that they are not held for purposes of revenge but to clarify responsibility. At these meetings the perpetrator must confess to wrongdoing; assume sole responsibility, with *no excuses;* and apologize to the victim.

Confronting the Shame of Having Had a Mental Disorder

Recovering patients, in the last stages of their therapy, often express feelings of profound shame about having had a mental disorder. They are regretful about the time lost, which may amount to many years. They feel that they are behind others their own age as a result of being "out sick" for so long, and worry that they will never "catch up" in the sense of achieving emotional maturity, job or career development, social skills, and romance.

All of these issues must be dealt with before therapy can be considered complete. People who have recovered from a mental illness need to be reminded of their enormous achievement, and the unusual and valuable education they have acquired in the therapeutic process. Generally, it is helpful if a therapist, or a member of the person's family, can coach them on how to deal with issues that may now arise in the real world, to role-play solutions, and to follow up with a review on how the person fared with putting the strategy into practice.

Self-help groups exist for people who have experienced mental illness and have recovered but still are left with feelings of low self-esteem due to their illness. If the person has been hospitalized in a psychiatric facility, the stigma and accompanying feelings of anger and shame are intensified. Some hospitals even offer post-discharge meetings to cope with these issues.

Blaming

The issue of why a person became ill in the first place is something that most recovered people think about occasionally. However, when someone is preoccupied with thoughts of who to blame, they are bound to act such thoughts out—either against others or against themselves. If they continue to blame themselves for lack of an apparent villain, they may sabotage their own success.

Self-blame is caused by feelings that the individual doesn't really deserve to recover or to be treated as a success. Beneath successful behavior toward others may lurk the uneasy feeling that "If they really knew who I have been, and who I may be [a fraud], they would lose all respect for me." As self-esteem increases, this fear will diminish.

A major issue for the recovering cutter, as for persons recovering from other mental disorders, is a lack of appreciation for just how much they have been through and what they have overcome. Self-confidence can develop when friends and family take note of this achievement. Letting go of blame—whether of oneself or others—is an important aspect of the healing process.

The Fear of Incomplete Analysis

Most of us believe that we will never understand ourselves completely. People who have recovered from psychiatric problems sometimes are concerned that if certain unconscious insights have not been uncovered, they will remain vulnerable to more problems or even to a relapse. This is a two-sided issue. If there *are* serious feelings that have not yet been explored or interpreted, they may indeed prevent permanent recovery, since the individual will not be aware of behaviors or situations that reflect past, destructive experiences.

On the other hand, over-analysis can lead to a person becoming so preoccupied that the search turns into a useless obsession, even inducing problems that did not exist before. Endless speculation about oneself creates a style of self-absorption or narcissism that produces social penalties. After the intense experience of self-exploration provided by therapy, the recovered cutter should remember that perfection is never a healthy goal, even in recovery.

The Scars

Unlike many psychiatric and psychological disorders, cutting leaves scars, literally. This is permanent proof that the person had the disorder. Anorexics, after they have gained their weight and recovered, look like anybody else. They may be left with an excessive fear of becoming overweight, and keep themselves a bit too thin, along with other idiosyncratic eating patterns. But this fact is not as obvious as the actual scars that recovered cutters must contend with.

There are only a limited number of explanations that the former cutter can make up to explain away such scars. Some include in-line skating accidents or skateboard mishaps, but even these are limited to appropriate places on the body.

Scars, then, become the most visible and explicit stigma for the recovered cutter to deal with. One has to choose between the deceptive—"I hung out with a group of kids who were into this crazy scarmaking" (disassociating oneself from its former meaning)—or telling the truth. The truth is often the best explanation, though the information should be limited.

When a person is referring honestly to the origins of scars, it is important that the interrogator does not merely pose questions in order to gratify their own curiosity. Answering questions like, "Did it hurt?" or, "Did you know what you were doing to yourself?" leave the recovered cutter feeling humiliated and exposed, and often create tensions that resemble old feelings and anxieties.

An exception might be made for a patient's long-term best friend, fiancé, or spouse. Even then, any questions should be minimal, unless the desire to make the disclosure comes from the former self-mutilator herself; otherwise, the information is none of the questioner's business. A good way to respond to such questions or offer an explanation is to say, "These are scars from a very painful time in my life. I'm grateful that it's in the past." Within a really close relationship, of course, increased sharing should be a natural and gradual process.

The Persistence of Hereditary and/or Chemical Disturbances

People who are blessed with very calm nervous systems, who come from families with little or no history of mental illness, are the least likely to develop mental or emotional disorders. Family life has a powerful influence on a child's developing emotional stability. Yet in the same family we often see one child who grows up with relatively few emotional problems while another develops significantly greater problems and is diagnosed as mentally ill.

There are some families in which all the children have severe psychiatric problems.

The recovered cutter not only retains her physical scars but the neurochemical/hereditary factors that contributed toward her predisposition to become mentally ill in the first place. Patients who are put on medication always ask me, before starting it, "Will I have to be on this for the rest of my life?" I have no way of knowing for certain, nor does anyone else. Some people use medication for a year or two, to help overcome their "mental crisis period," and then can stop using it. Others find that when they do discontinue their medication, overwhelmingly painful feelings return. If these are not reported promptly, cutting or other symptoms can reoccur. In such a case, the person will need to be on medication for an open-ended period of time.

Individuals who have recovered from their symptoms do not "recover" from their chemistry. Even if they have discontinued their medication and feel that they can do so without experiencing abnormal emotional pain, they still find themselves wondering whether they remain vulnerable to relapse due to their nervous system.

I usually explain that each of us develops a way of coping with emotional pain, whether it's a **safe** way—getting lost in a hobby, workaholic behavior, and so on—or an **unsafe** way—impairing or destructive behaviors, cutting, anorexia, alcoholism, and many other "choices." When the pressures and problems subside, we are freer to give up our unsafe coping mechanisms. Some can simply be relinquished; others may require treatment in order to give them up.

When someone has overcome one of the unsafe coping behaviors, like cutting, and is considered recovered, some future overwhelming event or catastrophe *might* produce a short temporary relapse. The likelihood of this is greater if the person has "vulnerable" chemistry. But the more complete the treatment, the recovery, and the family support available, the less likely the relapse, despite this unchanged hereditary chemistry.

Medication and Self-Esteem

For the recovered cutter who continues to have to use medication because without it she had relapsed either into cutting or into other behavioral problems such as depression or anxiety disorder, special issues have to be addressed.

"Can I call myself recovered if I have to stay on medication until God-knows-when?"

This question comes up often because the recovered cutter has a major issue involving self-esteem. One does not recover from one's heredity. If medication is required to normalize hereditary/chemical problems, the patient needs to understand that we are maintaining a normalization of her nervous system, but that she still has been victorious in defeating the symptoms generated by this genetic impairment.

Medication alone "cures" very few behavioral psychiatric problems, only those that are purely neurological in origin. Cutting is not in this category. When medication alone, or medication with a minimum of psychotherapy, is used to treat these symptoms, a relapse is more likely for several reasons: people miss the symptoms (even if they are the self-infliction of pain) that they have used to soften unbearable feelings. They most often need a therapist to help them let go of, or mourn the loss of these "loyal" and familiar symptoms. If they were treated only with medication, usually when they stop taking the medication that was relieving their need to experience or perform their symptoms, those symptoms will return.

Treatment involves an exchange. If the patient is experiencing a form of relief from her unwanted feelings by using a symptom (what we call **symptomatic relief**), someone will have to give her a compensating way of obtaining relief from the unwanted feelings. This compensation may be a different behavior, and/or a different quality of relationship with one or more other people (especially in cases where she is feeling alone, unable to trust and depend upon another). Medication alone does not satisfy either of these two issues. *A helping relationship must be added to the mix.*

When the patient has overcome her problems, using both psychotherapy and medication, she needs to receive recognition for having used the therapeutic relationship to find and accept a healthy alternative to her "symptomatic solution" for her unbearable feelings. The medication must be credited for freeing her from anxious, irritable, fearful, and depressed feelings that crippled her ability to use therapy. But she also is realistically entitled to credit for struggling through the unfamiliar emotional territory she has crossed on her way to recovery, as well as for her refusal to give in to the temptation to slip back to her familiar "old friend," the symptom.

It is this recognition—by her family, friends, and therapist—that supports the patient's newfound self-esteem. Parents and friends should certainly feel free to make positive comments: "Beth, you've been so brave to make this change," or, "I'm glad you've been telling me how you really feel—I know your recovery wasn't easy. I'm so proud of you."

It is important that the patient understands that the continuing use of medication is simply a regulating or normalizing device she is using as she might for any chronic illness. The medicine acts as a general chemical support. The changes were made by *her as a person,* not created by the medication.

Outgrowing Old Attitudes Toward One's Self

When the old symptoms have been eliminated and other external social behaviors and relationships with one's family improved, the self-mutilator would seem to have recovered. But there is still one more important change that must occur. That change involves the value that the person places upon her own self, her personality and character traits.

When someone begins treatment, I generally ask, "How do you feel about yourself?"

"What do you mean?" is the usual response.

"Do you think that you're smart, pretty, clever, interesting, patient, generous, caring, tough, likable, thoughtful, stubborn, or any other traits you'd like to throw in?"

In the early stages of treatment, I get the same profile of answers. I get a yes to "caring" and "stubborn," and a no to the rest of them. Some patients alter my list, including "boring, ugly, stupid, selfish, unlikable," among other negatives. Some include "tough" as an attribute that they possess.

Toward the conclusion of treatment, we take stock again, and the overall picture is much more positive.

The most significant comments that patients make about changes in themselves concern feelings they lived with all the time and that they now don't experience any more. These are best summed up by one girl who stated, "I used to always feel empty, like there were no words or ideas in my head. I would look in the mirror and find, in my reflection, a stranger. It was hard for me to care about that stranger. Now I feel that I know myself, and I *do* care."

What this young girl is saying refers to the change she feels about her *sense of identity*. Over the course of treatment, she learned a new language which enabled her to think about herself and express herself, and eventually to believe in what she was saying. In effect she is saying, "I didn't used to feel like I had a self. Now I do."

Regret

Regret is related to blame but even more to frustration. "How could I have done this to myself? I must have been crazy. Look at these scars! I'll have to get a plastic surgeon to remove some of them. I used to be so proud of them—they showed I could take pain. Now I want to throw up when I look at them. I hate taking baths. At least in the shower I don't have to really look at my skin."

The regrets expressed by many ex-cutters are interwoven between the general state of illness they experienced, and the physical confrontation of the scars. It becomes important here to deal with the *relationship* between blaming, regret, and the scars themselves.

The key here is for all those who are involved to help the recovering cutter forgive herself for making an honest attempt to find a solution, no matter how maladaptive it turned out to be and finally how obsolete it became upon recovery. Again, positive comments from friends and family can be an invaluable source of validation. The helping person can be direct in their support: "Beth, I hope you don't blame yourself for everything you've been through. I know your cutting was an attempt to solve a problem you didn't understand."

Individuals who "adapt," as children, to unbearable feelings, and dysfunctional aspects of their family, by employing what later becomes termed **psychologically disordered behavior**, upon recovery may have a hard time forgiving themselves. It becomes a major task for those helping them to convince them that they simply did the best they could under difficult circumstances, with no trustworthy guidance available at the time.

The Family's Recovery

The aftermath of the cutter's recovery varies greatly. Some families find the nature of the causes (especially incest) reason for divorce or breakup, whereas others remain in a state of apprehension, wondering when the illness will strike again. "Has it gone underground temporarily, or is she really over it?" one mother asked me anxiously. In a way, the family's reaction to recovery is often similar to the doctor's declaration after cancer surgery. "We got it all," says the doctor, "but we'll know for sure if it doesn't reappear for seven years."

If the family reacts to the recovered cutter as if she may relapse at any time, they are emphasizing their alienation from her. They are almost watching her from afar. Earlier, we saw how a failure in the attachment-dependency-trust axis can erode security in the family relationship. Success in these areas leads to incorporating family values and developing and maintaining feelings of security. Watching one's daughter suspiciously after recovery produces a separation, a suspicion, almost a paranoia, on the part of parents toward their child.

It is unrealistic to expect parents to forget the terror and heartbreak that they have been through as a result of their daughter's (or son's) illness; but improved communication and closeness—rather than watchfulness—will slowly erase these fearful feelings.

I am of course recommending behaviors and attitudes suitable for families when recovery does seem to have taken place, and not while the illness is still active.

Each family needs to examine the past and understand, *undefensively,* what went wrong for their child. Like the recovered cutter, family members have to deal with events and relationships at an earlier time in the family's history that blocked the parents from extending the invitation and the emotional safety to the child to communicate his or her feelings. Such a climate would have eliminated the development of the illness in most cases.

This kind of exercise is useful for the family in that they have to remain vigilant about the reoccurrence of the **family's dysfunction** instead of the child's illness. In this way, they create and maintain dialogue and closeness within the family, instead of fear and suspicion.

The most important family behavior is **communication**. Ask yourself the following questions:

- Do I sort out my feelings before I speak?
- Do I take responsibility for how I affect others?
- Do I deal directly with each family member in a considerate manner?
- Do I apologize when I'm wrong?
- Am I honest in expressing what I want and need from other family members?

These healthy behaviors were probably not role-modeled for parents in their *own* families, so they should be sure to get professional guidance if such changes are too difficult for them to achieve or maintain alone.

Warning signs of relapse include a renewed sense of isolation or lack of commitment on the part of the self-harmer; a superficially cheery manner that seems "unreal"; or an increase in excuse-making for withdrawing from normal activities.

Regaining One's Lost Social Place

It is typical for the recovering cutter to feel disheartened at times, complaining: "Nobody calls me anymore. When I call people I used to be friends with, they don't return my calls. Even when they do, which is rare, they just make light talk and get off the phone as soon as possible. I feel like I'll never have friends again."

In return, I might respond that "I think your peer community has learned over the last four years to become afraid of you. They've seen your scars. Apparently, your family, in their own despair, have turned to their friends, some of whom are your friends' parents, and word got around. My guess is that at first you were seen as suicidal, then after a while people began to see these repeated attempts at 'suicide' as frighteningly crazy."

I have heard of parents telling their own children to stay away from another child in the community who exhibited signs of emotional problems or mental illness. They may have been afraid that the illness, especially in the case of destructive acts, would be "catching," or at least influence their own children negatively.

Aside from parental influence, peer pressure develops to stay away from cutters because they have mental problems (especially if these last for years). People may feel that their own esteem in the peer group would be lowered if they are seen hanging around with a self-mutilator.

Finally, there's the individual friend's fear that the cutter is "lost to them" by becoming unpredictable. Her "mystery behavior" frightens them. They have been frightened of her for years now; that's how they think of her. It's going to take a while to teach them, repeatedly, that the self-mutilating behavior is over.

I returned to my discouraged patient with some instructions. "You will have to indicate, to your chronically frightened community, even announce, 'Hey, I'm back! You don't have to be afraid of me anymore.' "

"Won't that sound even weirder? It might scare them further away from me."

"I'm suggesting that you say something like this in your own words, but playfully. I think you will have to disclose that the behavior that everyone understandably backed away from is long gone; over. That gives you a chance to tell your friends that you don't blame them for backing away from you."

In a session several weeks later she grumbled a bit in our discussion of her "social return."

"I've noticed," she began, "that for a while it did work. I called everybody again and again until I got return calls and even invitations to go out with my friends. It's still not the same as it used to be. If there are three of us going somewhere, two of them quickly jump in the front seat of the car, leaving me alone in the back. It's not that they don't talk to me at all, but they seem to have so much more in common with each other—stuff that happened when I was sick, guys they met when I was 'out of it'—so that I still feel left out."

"When we started this 'social reentry' program, your friends weren't returning your calls. Now you're at a disadvantage in terms of social information and inclusion in discussions. It doesn't sound great, but it does sound like a lot of progress."

"Yeah." She nodded grudgingly.

The Future: Patience with Process and Progress

It takes only an instant to cut yourself. Cutters learn to expect instantaneous relief; they have no faith in gradual change. They feel that if a change does not take place *now*, then it will never occur. As one patient commented to me, "You often talk about the gradual progress I'm making. The trouble with thinking about the meantime, while I'm waiting to complete my recovery, is that the 'meantime' is such a *mean time*."

A major part of helping a self-mutilator involves remaining realistically encouraging and realistically complimentary. These positive but realistic responses provide a milepost, a finite point where a **bit of completion** has occurred. When one is emotionally separate, it is difficult to experience achievement or change because there is no one to verify it, nobody one has trust in. The concept of a slow process throws most cutters into despair. Once they have established the attachment-trust-dependency axis mentioned throughout this book, they can use a helping person to calm them down, allowing for the *mean time* to elapse while they recover.

EPILOGUE

If you read this book because you discovered that someone near and dear to you has been harming herself, you probably have been feeling worried, frustrated, angry, and maybe guilty, frightened, and confused. Surely you've said to yourself, "This is crazy. Why would anyone do this to herself?" I hope this book has cleared up some of those feelings and helped to answer your question. The person may even be angry with you for your new understanding of her pain. This will pass.

If you read this book because you are horrified by and curious about this kind of behavior, I hope you are now able to see the person beyond the behavior and understand that this is a curable disorder.

At one time or another in our lives, we have all experienced feelings or thoughts that have frightened us. Forgetting about them only invites further self-doubt. Instead, explore them.

For those of you who have read this book because you suffer from this malady, either by itself or accompanied by other kinds of impairing pain, you have the most difficult task ahead. You have a new language to learn, that of self-expression and reflection. In addition, you will have to take a risk that feels like free fall: first, the unfamiliar feelings, which are often painful, when forming words out of these feelings; and then finding someone who can help you, and entrusting them with your most private thoughts and feelings. The language of cutting, writing with your own blood as the ink, a blade as the pen, must be relinquished, replaced by *words,* spoken to that trusted person. Until now, your privacy and your secrecy have been your best friends. You will need to exchange them for one new friend, followed by others.

RECOMMENDED READINGS
ON SELF-MUTILATION

Alderman, T. *The Scarred Soul: Understanding and Ending Self-Inflicted Violence.* Oakland: New Harbinger, 1997.

Favazza, A. R. *Bodies Under Siege: Self Mutilation and Body Modification in Culture and Psychiatry.* 2nd ed. Baltimore: Johns Hopkins University Press, 1996.

Hawton, K. "Self-Cutting: Can It Be Prevented?" In K. Hawton and P. J. Crown, eds., *Dilemmas and Difficulties in the Management of Psychiatric Patients.* Oxford: Oxford University Press, 1990.

Heubner, Hans. *Endorphins and Anorexia.* New York: W. W. Norton, 1994.

Kernberg, O. F. *Severe Personality Disorders: Psychotherapeutic Strategies.* New Haven: Yale University Press, 1986.

Levenkron, S. *Obsessive-Compulsive Disorders.* New York: Warner Books, 1991.

———. *The Luckiest Girl in the World.* New York: Scribner, 1997.

———. *Treating and Overcoming Anorexia Nervosa.* 2nd ed. New York: Warner Books, 1997.

256   RECOMMENDED READINGS

Luiselli, J. K., J. L. Matson, and N. N. Singh, eds. *Self-Injurious Behavior: Analysis, Assessment, and Treatment.* New York: Springer-Verlag, 1992.

Miller, D. *Women Who Hurt Themselves: A Book of Hope and Understanding.* New York: Basic Books, 1994.

Pipher, M. *Reviving Ophelia: Saving the Selves of Adolescent Girls.* New York: Ballantine Books, 1994.

Walsh, B. W., and P. M. Rosen. *Self-Mutilation: Theory, Research, and Treatment.* New York: Guilford Press, 1988.

OTHER RESOURCES

Understanding Self-Injury: A Workbook for Adults. Helps survivors understand self-destructive behaviors and explore alternatives via writing and drawing exercises. To order, send $10 for the workbook, plus $1 for shipping and handling, to:

> Pittsburgh Action Against Rape
> 81 South 19th St.
> Pittsburgh, PA 15203-1852

Bulk discounts are available.

> The Cutting Edge
> P.O. Box 20819
> Cleveland, OH 44120

A self-injury newsletter.

SAFE Alternatives at Rock Creek Center: 1-800-DONTCUT. Provides information and referrals; sends out a really good information packet on request.

> S.A.F.E. (Self Abuse Finally Ends)
> 659 Dundas Street
> London, Ontario
> Canada N5W 2Z1

INDEX